GOD'S WORDS FOR LIFE

Daily Words of
Encouragement for Men

A DEVOTIONAL AND STUDY GUIDE BY

KEVIN S. LEE

Copyright © 2009 by Kevin S. Lee

God's Words for life
Daily Words of Encouragement for Men
by Kevin S. Lee

Printed in the United States of America

ISBN 978-1-60791-896-7

www.xulonpress.com

Table of Contents

INTRODUCTION

I grew up in a non-Christian home. I was not raised in church or Sunday school. I spent most of my life on the east coast – New York City, Pittsburgh, Pa, and the Washington metropolitan area. I had a fairly good life growing up. At times, I lived in the inner city and in suburban areas. I experienced the best and worst of both worlds. But, I always remember feeling "empty." I always felt like I was missing something in my life. There wasn't any academic achievement, sports accomplishment, or words from my family that could fill the void. I had a good life, but I always wondered, "Why do I feel this way? Am I missing something?"

Many years later, while attending college in Boston, I met some Christian friends who invited me to their church one Sunday morning. As I recall, I had a wonderful time and at the end of the service, I prayed a prayer of faith and gave my life to God. During my sophomore year, I stumbled upon a Bible that someone had left behind in one of the empty dormitory rooms. I suppose it was there for me to discover. I began reading it regularly and several years later started attending church regularly too. My life was quite a journey over the next several years.

I encountered many challenges. Several family members died of cancer. My younger sister died in an automobile accident. My older brother announced that he decided to live a homosexual lifestyle. My parents divorced. I felt like my life was spiraling out of control. I needed something or someone to hold onto. At some point, I began a deep search to discover who this God really was. As I read the Bible, I discovered so many encouraging words. I discovered God's great love for me. Each day I read more and grew more encouraged. God's Word addressed every challenge I encountered.

Many years later, I moved from the east coast to California. On the west coast, I experienced my great spiritual awakening. After working in the legal profession for many years, I began to sense God tugging on my heart for full-time vocational ministry. With an ever-increasing desire to know God, I began serving as the men's ministry leader at my church, Abundant Life Christian Fellowship, Mountain View, Ca. God gave me a passion to reach lost and hurting men. Several years later, I sensed a calling to enter seminary to prepare to work as a pastor in the local church. Following graduation, I joined staff at my church where I now serve as the men's pastor.

As a men's pastor, I know firsthand how God's Word can bring change. He changed my life in a powerful way. I experienced God's transformative power in ways I never thought possible. I experienced a break-thru in the areas of pride, arrogance, jealousy, lust, and more. It's only through this change that He has allowed me to minister to men in the local church. As a result, I now minister to and counsel men struggling with pride, anger, depression, lust, pornography, sexual abuse, addiction, divorce, death, marital problems, and a host of other issues. I realize that men struggle with a lot of different issues at home, work, and in life everyday. I also realize that these issues are often frustrating, discouraging, and downright depressing. Thus, it's my contention that men need daily encouragement to stay on track. I seek to bring encouragement to all men through this book.

God's Words for Life draws on the rich insights from a wide array of encouraging stories, which are designed to reach men of all ages and from all walks of life. Men will sit down and read stories that they can relate to. Men are also able to savor the insight that only God's Word can bring through an affirmation, study questions, meditate verse, and reflection section, which accompany each devotional. Day by day, these stories and study tools will encourage and challenge every man to be the man God has called him to be.

DEDICATION

Dedicated to my wife, Connie.

You have come alongside, partnered, and
cheered for me.
You always loved me unconditionally.

When I needed a push you were there.
You have valued me and my gifts.
You have been my best friend.
You have stood beside me.
You are my heart.

You have encouraged me to open doors
that I was uncertain could open.
You have dared me to dream big dreams.
My world is better because of you.
My life is easier because of you.
I am a better man because of you.

This book wouldn't exist without you.
I love you with all of my heart.
Te Amo Mi Amour

WITH GRATITUDE

I want to say thanks to my friends Thomas Green and Natasha Duncan for their prayers. I couldn't have written this book without God's direction. I also would like to say thanks to Emily Chow, Brian Murphy, Eric Simms, Jacqueline Perry, Brian Person, and other family and friends for their encouragement and guidance with this book. The editorial skills of each person helped to bring *God's Word's for Life* to its finished state.

IMPOSSIBLE IS NOTHING

Jesus replied, "What is impossible with men
is possible with God." Luke 18:27

Have you ever faced circumstances that seemed utterly overwhelming? A situation that you thought was nearly impossible to overcome? A moment where the odds were clearly not in your favor? When you had the deck stacked against you?

Well, many of us have faced (or are facing) these kinds of challenges in our life. We face these kinds of challenges in marriage, parenting, work, and a host of other areas. These challenges, some of life's most difficult moments, cause us to shut down, shut others out, hide, or run away to avoid something we can't handle.

The common reaction – avoidance – is most readily apparent when we are faced with circumstances that seem impossible to overcome. In these instances, our thoughts tend to lean toward taking matters into our own hands. And we try to solve the problem on our own by using our own wisdom. We consider the situation and ask ourselves, "What can I do to resolve it, overcome it, or fix it?" Oftentimes, doing things on our own only makes things worse.

But, what appears like a boulder in man's eyes is nothing more than a pebble to God. Our great Father in Heaven is a Way Maker. (Isa. 43:16, 19) He can move mountains right before our eyes. He is the One and Only who gives us strength to be overcomers so we are able to see our way through life's greatest challenges. The only thing He asks is that we trust Him to bring about the best possible outcome. And God's way offers the most desirable outcome for our life. Any attempt we might make to bring about change in our life is futile.

God, however, can change our circumstances in the blink of an eye. He simply wants us to invite Him to do the impossible. He wants us to allow Him to work out things so that His name is glorified. When we trust Him, and surrender every detail of the challenge to Him, then He is in the best position to make what seemed impossible possible in our life.

Affirmation

God, Nothing is Impossible when:
- I have been unjustly fired and I need a job
- I feel like a failure to my wife and kids
- I am experiencing unbearable health issues
- I desire to overcome my addiction
- I devote my life completely to you

Meditation Verse

"[He] is able to do immeasurably more than all we ask or imagine, according to his power that is at work within us, to him be glory in the church and in Jesus Christ throughout all generations, for ever and ever! Amen." Ephesians 3:20-21

Discussion Questions
1. Have you ever faced an impossible situation in which you responded poorly? You stressed,

ran away, etc.? How would you respond differently if you had to face that situation again with God?

2. Are you facing a difficult life situation right now? What do you believe is the best way to handle it? Have you shared this situation with anyone?

3. How do you think God would want you to handle difficult circumstances that arise in life? What is the biblical basis for your response?

Prayer

Father in heaven, you know every detail of my life. You know what's going on right now as I lift this prayer up to you. I confess Lord that I cannot work out my circumstances alone. I need your help. I know that you are a Way Maker. You make a way where I cannot see one. So I ask you to move in a mighty way in my life today. I pray that you would make the impossible possible and help me to overcome overwhelming odds. I trust and believe that all things are possible through you who give me strength. In Jesus' name. Amen.

Reflection

_____

_____

_____

_____

_____

ALL FOR YOU

"And whatever you do, whether in word or
deed, do it all in the name of the
Lord Jesus, giving thanks to God the Father
through him." Colossians 3:17

In Colossians, Paul wrote to the church during
his first imprisonment in Rome. He spent at least two
years under house arrest. Imprisonment, however,
was not Paul's only plight. During his life, he was
scorned, stoned, treated with contempt, and faced
illness. (Acts 16:22 et seq.; Galatians 4)

Despite his circumstances, Paul boldly professed
the gospel wherever he traveled. On one occasion,
he wrote, "As you know, it was because of an illness
that I first preached the gospel to you." (Gal. 4:13)
He wrote on other occasions from prison and encouraged others. (See Philippians)

Paul wasn't shy about lifting up God's name in
his life. He said, "I eagerly expect and hope that I
will in no way be ashamed, but will have sufficient
courage so that now as always Christ will be exalted
in my body whether by life or death." (Phil. 1:20) Not
only did he believe it for his life, but he encouraged
others to do the same. Paul said, "Fight the good fight
of faith. Take hold of eternal life to which you were
called when you made your confession in the presence of witnesses." (1 Tim. 6:12)

We should take heed of Paul's words and actions.
He suffered more hardship and pain than most of us

will encounter in a lifetime. Despite his suffering, he still rejoiced in the Lord and was content in his circumstances. So why do we complain when our challenges are so small in comparison?

Since most of our lives have not been nearly as difficult as Paul's, shouldn't this be all the more reason for our lives to glorify Him? Shouldn't you just give Him thanks right now for your family, home, car, spouse, kids, job, school, etc? Everything we do, we do for the Lord. For without Him nothing else is possible. And, with him, "all things are possible." (Mark 10:27)

Are you making a concerted effort to give God thanks through your every word and deed? Are you faithfully serving Him despite challenging circumstances in your life? God wants to be your all-in-all, but He wants you to turn to Him and say, "All for you, Lord." God is worthy of all praise. "To him be honor and might forever. Amen." (1 Timothy 6:16)

Affirmation

Lord, I will remember All for You when:
- I want to do something hurtful to others
- I have been abused, neglected, or mistreated
- Others are saying hurtful things about me
- I don't think I can take life's pressures anymore
- I am feeling low, beat down, and defeated

Meditation Verse

"Consider it pure joy when you face trials of many kinds, because you know that the testing of your faith develops perseverance. Perseverance must finish its work so that you may be mature and complete, not lacking anything." James 1:2-4

Discussion Questions

1. Identify three areas of your life where you believe you are being tested? How are you dealing with your circumstances? If you are struggling, how can you improve your response?
2. How did Paul handle difficult situations? (See Paul's epistles)
3. Have you given thanks to God lately? Consider all you have to be thankful for and share those thoughts with someone or in a small group. How can you show God how grateful you are everyday?

Prayer

Lord Jesus, I am pressed, not crushed, persecuted, not abandoned, struck down, but not destroyed. I praise you for how you have never left me or forsaken me. Despite the difficulties I face in this world, you have always been there for me. I thank you because there is protection underneath the shadow of your wing. I am thankful that it's you who I run to – my refuge, my fortress. I am thankful that you are God all by yourself. There is none like you. I will praise your name despite the challenges that are confronting me. In Jesus' name. Amen.

Reflection

_____

_____

_____

_____

_____

WHAT MATTERS MOST

"The only thing that counts is faith
expressing itself through love."
Galatians 5:6

A lot of people get consumed with the things of
this world. Many people are busy trying to get ahead
at work – seeking a new job title, more pay, etc. Many
are busy caring for family – a spouse, child(ren),
elder parent, or other loved ones or trying to keep up
with the Jones' – buying a big house, new car, etc.
You name it, we are busy doing it. Now, all of these
things are fine if pursued in the right spirit. But, what
is not good is overindulging in anything and making
people or "things" a priority before God.

At times, life stuff – both good and bad things
– can be a distraction. Having the wrong focus can
cause you to fail to realize what God wants most from
you. In Exodus 20:3, the Bible says: "You shall have
no other gods before me." God wants us to prosper in
the world, but not to our own detriment. He doesn't
want us to be so preoccupied with worldly things that
we put Him in the back seat of our life. He doesn't
want us to fly our own plane and have him come
along as our co-pilot. No, God wants to be the pilot
who flies the plane that consistently arrives for a safe
landing. He wants you to give Him your undivided
attention.

The Bible tells us that we are called to be free.
(Gal. 5:1) Your freedom comes from God's gift

of grace, which He gives freely. The Lord doesn't want you to use your freedom in a sinful way. To the contrary, He has called you to live a life of love. "The entire law is summed up in a single command: 'Love your neighbor as yourself." (Gal. 5:14) This life is lived by exuding the "fruit of the Spirit," (Gal. 5:22), the first of which is love. Paul says in Galatians that the only thing that counts in God's eyes is that we live a life of love through faith in Him. (Gal. 5:7) What matters most to God is that we put nothing before Him and live a life pleasing to Him.

Take a moment and be honest with yourself. Do you need to re-adjust your focus? Do you have things that are competing for your time with God? What is taking up the god-place in your life? What is causing you to place God in the second seat? What is keeping you from giving Him the undivided attention He deserves?

Affirmation
God, What Matters Most is:
- That I exercise my faith everyday
- That I love you with all of my heart
- That I put no other gods before you
- That I am not consumed with worldly things
- My personal relationship with Jesus Christ

Meditation Verse
"Love is patient, love is kind…It always protects, always trusts, always hopes, always perseveres. Love never fails." 1 Cor. 13:4-8

Discussion Questions

1. What Bible character do you admire the most? How did s/he live an authentic Christian life? How did s/he make God a priority? How can you do the same?

2. Are you living a faithful life? How do you know you are being faithful? What keeps you from being distracted by worldly things? Explain.

3. What things are taking up the god-places in your life? How do you identify them? How can you effectively eliminate the god-place(s) in your life?

Prayer

Jehovah God, you have been such a tremendous blessing to me. You have saved me and kept my feet from stumbling. You have seen me through difficult times when I couldn't even walk on my own. During those times, I know you carried me. You have always been with me. Therefore, I will praise you everyday that I am on this side of heaven. I will worship you and dance like David danced. I will take the seed you planted in me and live it out in service to you. I honor you. In Jesus' name. Amen.

Reflection

_____

_____

_____

_____

No More Worry

"Do not worry about tomorrow, for
tomorrow will worry about itself.
Each day has enough trouble of its own."
Matthew 6:34

Matthew tells us that you can be sure you will have trouble in this world. (Matt. 6:34) If you have not experienced trouble in your life just keep on living and it's bound to find you. Many people have experienced (or are experiencing) trouble. Perhaps, it's a layoff from work, a financial difficulty, the loss of a loved one, an illness, a broken relationship, or some other challenging situation. You don't have to live too long to realize that life will throw you many curve balls. It's not always easy. And, to make matters worse, a lot of life's challenges can cause you to struggle emotionally – to feel angry, anxious, bitter, depressed, frustrated, hopeless, or even suicidal.

The good news is that you don't have to worry about life, what you will eat, drink, or wear. (Matt. 6:25) You don't need to be anxious or worry about anything because God has everything under control. When you worry, you tell God that you're not sure He can really handle everything. You say, "God, I know you created the universe. And, I know that you created every living creature on this earth. (Gen. 1:21, 27) And, I know that you own cattle on a thousand hills. (Ps. 50:10) But, I am not sure you can handle this one little thing that's got me all worried and stressed." Sounds rather ridiculous, huh?

Well, in our humanness it seems to make sense for us to try to work things out on our own. We certainly can get some results that way. And, many of us have adopted this approach at some point in life. The reality, though, is that you won't get God's results by doing it your way. The Lord wants you to rely on Him and realize that you don't have to worry about anything today or tomorrow because His plan has been set before even time began. (Jer. 29:11) God already knows the outcome of every situation. He wants you to understand that His plan is far greater than anything you could ever conceive of in your mind. Consequently, God's desire is that you focus on today, not tomorrow. Seek first His kingdom and His righteousness, knowing that all else will be given to you. (Matt. 6:33)

Do you know that worrying is about you, not God? Instead of being self-centered why don't you release to Him whatever it is that's causing you to worry? It's a matter of faith and trust, and God doesn't want you to worry about anything.

Affirmation

Lord, No More Worry:
- When I am feeling uncertain about life
- When things seem to be pretty hopeless
- When there is no light at the end of the tunnel
- Because worrying can lead to other problems
- Because you guide me with your Word

Meditation Verse

"Search me, O God, and know my heart; test me and know my anxious thoughts. See if there is any offensive way in me, and lead me in the way everlasting." (Psalm 139:23-24)

Discussion Questions

1. Are you a worrier? What area(s) of worry do you struggle with the most? What do you believe is the root cause of your worrying? How can you worry less?
2. What are some practical ideas you can implement that will help you worry less? Exercise? Hobbies? Other? How can you become content in every situation?
3. What does the Bible say about worry and contentment?

Prayer

Father, I ask you to examine my heart. I realize that it's not a light matter when you examine me, but I do not want to be one who worries. Rather, I want to trust you completely. Worrying is an area of my life where I need to get a grip. Worrying is clear evidence of my lack of faith in the One who is the Source of strength. I ask that you would strengthen me in this area. Make my weakness into strength. I trust you and believe in your name, Jesus. Amen.

Reflection

_____

_____

_____

_____

_____

THE LEAST IS THE GREATEST

"If anyone wants to be first, he must be the
very last, and servant of all." Mark 9:35

Have you ever noticed how people want to always
be first in line? Some people will camp out overnight
to get the first tickets for the concert that is sure to
be sold out. Some get advance purchase tickets for
shows, sporting events, etc., to be able to sit in the
front row. And many will wait at the front door of
the mall until it opens to be able to be first to buy
the items on sale or cut in line when seeing someone
familiar despite all the folks standing in the long line.
We all sometimes have a desire to be first in line. It
makes us feel important. But, this is not a value that
Jesus embraced.

Jesus said that the first shall be last and the last
shall be first. (Mark 9:35) He spoke these words to
His disciples who were arguing about who is the
greatest. He then took a little child in his arms and
stood among them saying, "Whoever welcomes one
of these little children in my name welcomes me."
(Mark 9:36) Jesus knew that greatness came through
innocence and humility. And, in order to be first in
line, you must assume this kind of posture in life.

Jesus does not want you to race through life
consumed with your own self importance or putting
yourself in a place where you think you should be.
Rather, His desire is that you trust the One that you
cannot see, but who knows what's best for your life.

The Bible says, "Do nothing out of selfish ambition or vain conceit, but in humility consider others better than yourself." (Phil.2:3) The greatest among you should be like the youngest, and the one who rules should be like the one who serves. (Luke 22:26) God's plan for our lives is often times counterintuitive. It goes against the grain of our thinking. But, in the end it's the best way for us to live.

Affirmation

Lord, The Least is the Greatest:

- When I am tempted to step on others to get ahead
- When I feel consumed by my own self-importance
- When others waiting behind me have greater needs
- When I need a reminder to be more Christ-like
- Because you have set the example for this kind of life

Meditation Verse

"[W]hoever wants to be great among you must be your servant, and whoever wants to be first must be slave to all." Mark 10:43

Discussion Questions

1. Do you remember when you cut in line as a child? Do you still do that in some ways as an adult? Take an inventory of your life. Where do you want to be ahead of others?

2. Are you consumed with your own self-importance? Do you consider yourself before the needs other? If so, how can you re-adjust your thinking?

3. What does the Bible say about servanthood? What biblical passages come to mind that help you understand the values that Jesus shared about being a humble servant? What area(s) of your life do you need to be more child-like?

Prayer

Father, in the name of Jesus, I pray that you would make me more like you. I do not want to be caught up in my own self-importance. I know that is not what you want from me. I can be self-centered. When I am, I get out of your will for my life. I do not want to cut people off or have to be seen or heard. Rather, I'd like to take the proper place in life – behind others with greater needs. Lord, your ways are not my ways. Your thoughts are not my thoughts. Today, right now, I'd like to trade in what I desire for what you have for me. Blessed be your name. Amen.

Reflection

_____

_____

_____

_____

_____

GET UP AND GO

"He got up and went to His Father."
Luke 15:30

Sin is a horrible thing. Many of us can remember some sin in our past – an act of sexual impurity, lying, stealing, or another sin. You told yourself, "I can't believe I did that!" Or you might have even beaten yourself up over past mistakes. Sometimes, our old ways can keep us bound such that we don't go to church or spend time with people who can help us overcome issues from the past. As a result, we end up harboring feelings of guilt, shame, and other emotions that keep us stuck and feeling sorry for ourselves.

But, God through His son Jesus Christ, who has compassion for each of us, is waiting with open arms. He is waiting for you to come to your senses and return home. He wants you to come to Him and say, "Father, I have sinned against heaven and you." (Luke 15:18) I have failed myself and, perhaps, others in my life. I confess that I cannot live without you. I trade in my ways and come to you. Then, God, who is filled with great mercy and compassion, turns to you and says, "My son, you are always with me and everything I have is yours." (Luke 15:31)

Aren't you glad you serve a God who doesn't hold your past against you? He stands ready to give you the best robe and shoes, and start a celebration for His son who was dead, but is now alive again. He was lost and now he is found. (Luke 15:24) Aren't you glad that despite what you've done God still loves you? Aren't you glad that despite how you look, feel, or what you think about yourself, God is still waiting for you to come home?

Perhaps, it's time for you to go to Him – fully surrendered. Maybe you've been away from church far too long or maybe some area of your life is misaligned with God's will. In either case, God is welcoming you home to celebrate! Are you ready to go to Him? Get up and go!

Affirmation

Father, I Get Up And Go:

- Because I am tired of being separated from you
- Because I desperately hunger for your love
- Despite my feelings of guilt or shame
- Because I need to be restored by your goodness
- Because I've been away from you for too long

Meditation Verse

"Come to me, all you who are weary and burdened, and I will give you rest. Take my yoke upon you and learn from me…For my yoke is easy and my burden is light." (Matt. 11:28-30)

Discussion Questions

1. Is there an area of your life where you feel stuck? Why do you feel stuck? How did you get stuck? How can you get unstuck?

2. What positive things did David do when he was dealing with sin in his past? (See Psalm 51) What happened when David did not deal with sin in his past? What were the consequences? Can you think of some biblical examples?

3. How can you (with God's help) make a shift from where you are to where God wants you to be? How can God help you get unstuck? Share your thoughts with someone or in a small group.

Prayer

Lord Jesus, you have made me into a new creation. I am not a product of my past emotions, feelings, hurts, or pains. I was made in newness once I accepted you as Lord and Savior in my life. I express this newness by living as a new creature in Christ Jesus. Thank you for your sacrifice on the cross for all of my sin – past, present, and future. I acknowledge that I need you to help me get unstuck. I need you to help me see that my identity is rooted in you, not my past. I love you Lord. Amen.

Reflection

_____

_____

_____

_____

_____

LESS IS MORE

"He must become greater; I must become less." (John 3:30)

The media sends us so many conflicting messages. The world tells us to buy the big car, the large house, the expensive clothes, etc. Television and radio ads entice you to buy the fancy car or truck so you can drive in comfort, the large home so you can have a lot of space, and to pursue a job that pays a lot of money so you can truly feel fulfilled. We are lured into dressing a certain way, looking a certain way, and acting a certain way, all in the name of success. The world tells us that when we have these things we've made it. We are successful.

Now, having all of these things is fine when kept in proper perspective, but many of us know that even with these things in our life, we can still feel uncomfortable, empty, unhappy, and alone. The problem begins when there is too much "us" in the equation and not enough "Him." It's really not a matter of what you have. Rather, it's a matter of who you have and who has you.

"The one who comes from above is above all; the one who is from the earth belongs to the earth, and speaks as one from the earth. The one who comes from heaven is above all." (John 3:31) God doesn't focus on success the way man does. He's not interested in your outer appearance, clothes or style, the type of car you drive, or house you live in. He looks at your heart. (I Sam. 16:7) He wants you to decrease in things that occupy or consume you – things you believe are important – and increase in the things of Him – prayer, Bible study, worship, etc. "The man who accepts this certifies that God is truthful." (3:33)

How are you doing in your relationship with Christ? Do you need to re-prioritize? Do you have some things that are causing an unnecessary clutter in your life or clouding how you see your relationship with God? Is He Lord over every area of your life? If not, what area(s) do you need to shrink down in the things of "you" and rise up in the things of "Him?"

Affirmation

Lord, Less is More:
- When I am tempted to buy a fancy car
- When I am seeking worldly patterns of success
- When I am seeking status in corporate America
- When I am seeking to impress others
- When I am devoted to following Jesus Christ

Meditation Verse

"Whoever claims to live in him must walk as Jesus did." (1 John 2:6)

Discussion Questions

1. What would you do if God instructed you to give up everything you have and follow Him? Would you hesitate? Would you delay?

Or, would you drop everything and obedi-
ently follow him? Be honest with yourself.
(See Luke 5:11)

2. How do you get to the point of obedience
   without second guessing God? (See Luke
   9:57)

3. In what areas do you need to shrink in your
   own self-thinking and increase in God-
   thinking? Have you confessed where you fall
   short? Explain.

Prayer

Oh God, I pray that you would fill me with your
Living Water. I want to drink from the fountain that
brings life to my body. Fill me so that the reservoir of
my heart overflows. I want to displace my thoughts
with thoughts of only you. I hunger and thirst for
righteousness. I seek not to impress others or live
according to the patterns of this world, but rather
according to your patterns for my life. I desire to
walk in your ways and be without stain or blemish.
I lift my head up to the hills to see where my help
comes from and I know it comes from you, Lord.
Blessings and honor to you. In Jesus' name. Amen.

Reflection

_____

_____

_____

_____

_____

SHOW ME FAVOR

"Surely, O Lord you bless the righteous,
you surround them with your favor as with a
shield." Psalm 5:12

Have you ever watched how a VIP gets special treatment? Whether it is a U.S. President, a professional athlete, a CEO, a public figure or official traveling with an entourage of some sort. The VIP's have doors opened for them or receive special treatment in some other way. Perhaps, you've experienced this type of treatment in your life like being moved to the front of a long line or given some other priority in a particular situation. If so, then you realize how much of a blessing it is to be treated that way.

Maybe though, you've also been exposed to the opposite. Perhaps, you've experienced humiliation, being shunned or treated with contempt, blackballed, or otherwise mistreated by others. The Apostle Paul had this experience. Although he sought to do good, he was scorned, stoned, and treated with contempt. (Acts 16:22) Paul definitely did not receive VIP treatment. (See Paul's life)

The good news, however, is that the Lord "will look on [you] with favor" when you do His will. (Lev. 26:9) You are a VIP to Him. And, because you are sons of the King of kings, he wants to show you favor, even if you've been mistreated. Even in distress, God wants you to seek His favor. (2 Ch. 33.12) Despite your circumstances, God wants to treat you like royalty. He wants you to know that you are special in His eyes because He created you... and everything He created is good. (Gen. 1:31) The amazing thing is that He gives you free access to His heavenly throne so you never have to feel rejected or humiliated. (John 8:36)

God wants you to experience His favor. He knows what it's like to feel rejected. (See Mark 14-16) Therefore, he understands your pain and has promised to surround you with favor by his mighty hand. This means that you don't have to worry about those who attempt to set you back. You can stand on His Word because He is your protection that surrounds you with His favor as with a shield. "May the favor of the Lord our God rest upon [you]." (Psalm 90:17)

Affirmation

Lord, Show Me Favor:

- When I am shunned, despised, or disrespected
- When I am feeling rejected by others
- In my home, workplace, and community
- So I can be a blessing to others
- So I can fulfill your purpose and plan for my life

Meditation Verse

"In the time of my favor I heard you, and in the day of salvation I helped you." 2 Cor. 6:2

Discussion Questions

1. Have you ever been left out or felt that way? Last one picked for the team or not selected at all? Overlooked at work? How did it make you feel? How did you deal with your feelings?

2. Think about a time when God showed you favor? How did you respond? Did you thank Him? How did His favor impact you then and now?

3. Consider biblical examples (Noah, Mary, others) who found favor in God's eyes? What did they do to receive His favor? Consider other verses which relate to God's favor. (2 Sam. 2:6; Prov. 8:30; Isa. 61; Zec. 11:7; Luke 4:19)

Prayer

I seek your favor, Lord. Blessed are those who are persecuted, and when people insult you, persecute you and falsely say all kinds of evil against you. I will yet rejoice and be glad because I know that you have a greater reward in heaven. If only I can persist and wait for your perfect timing, I know that you will rescue me. You are a help in my time of need. Lord, I pray that I might find continuous favor in your eyes. In Jesus' name. Amen.

Reflection

_____

_____

_____

_____

_____

THE MASTER'S PLAN

"No eye has seen, no ear has heard, no mind conceived what God has prepared for those who love him." 1 Cor. 2:9-10

Do you know that God has a plan for your life? Many Christians know He has a plan, but aren't certain exactly what the plan is. So, how do you discover His plan for your life? You want to receive His many blessings and you desire to do His will, but how do you know His will and put yourself in the best position to discover and carry it out?

God wants you to know . . . and He wants to tell you. But, how? Will He speak to you from a burning bush or from atop Mt. Sinai? Probably not. But He can speak to you when you are on your knees, standing, laying prostrate or seated, praying to discern His will. He can speak to you through the Bible while you are studying His Word. He can speak to you through another believer, a non-believer, or, if all else fails, a rock. He can use anything He likes to make His plan known to you. You just need to be available to hear and listen to what He has to say.

Once He reveals himself, you can rest assured that He only has good plans for you. (Jer. 29:11) And, whatever He's planning has far-reaching implications for your life. God's plan and purpose is much bigger than you can comprehend. Your mind is too small to grasp it. You must just meet Him, expecting to hear from Him, and ready to receive what He has to say. One thing is for sure, His plans are far better than anything you could think of in your own small mind. A great preacher once said, "If you want to make God laugh tell Him your plans."

"[W]hat may be known about God's plan is plain to them, because God has made it plain to them." (Rom. 1:19) He has made himself known to everyone so that "men are without excuse." (Rom. 1: 20) Have you discovered what God's plan is for your life?

Affirmation

I rely on The Master's Plan:
- For moments when I want to do things my way
- For my spouse, children, career, and life
- So that things will always turn out right
- So that all will go well with me and my family
- Because I serve a great and mighty God

Meditation Verse

"Many are the plans in a man's heart, but it is the Lord's purpose that prevails." (Prov. 19:21)

Discussion Questions

1. Have you ever made plans on your own that went well? You had some measure of success in something you did? Explain. Can you imagine those plans being even more successful had you given them over to the Lord?

2. Have you ever made plans that did not work out? What was the negative consequence of your failed plan? What steps would you take if you had a chance to do it over again? How can you avoid negative consequences of your thinking?

3. Consider several biblical characters that consulted with God and experienced His best, (See Nehemiah), or others who made their choice despite God's clear instruction? (See Jonah)

Prayer

Lord Jesus, I pray that you would order my steps because you have a good plan for my life. You know everything that will happen before it happens. You know about every detail of my life. I want to be in conformity with your plan so I can be in the center of your will. You are wonderful, awesome, marvelous, and majestic. Great is your love for me. I pray that I am able to show you the same love everyday of my life. I surrender my thoughts to you. I trade in my plans for yours. Lead me down the right path. I want to know the great things you have for me. In Jesus' name. Amen.

Reflection

_____

_____

_____

_____

RESHAPE MY HEART

"I will give you a new heart and put a new
spirit in you; I will remove from you
your heart of stone and give you a heart of
flesh." (Ezek. 36:26)

What is the condition of your heart? Is it soft
and pliable, filled with generosity, compassion, and
understanding? Is it tender, gentle, kind, and loving?
Or is it hard and frigid, filled with hostility, bitterness, anger, or rage? If it's the former, then God can
use you, and perhaps, already has. But, if you don't
like what you see, then you might need to make some
adjustments.

Think about it like this. A person has to go to
the doctor's office for an appointment. While there,
the doctor informs him that he has a heart problem.
Perhaps, there's a valve problem or some other
issue causing the heart to be weak or malfunction.
The doctor recommends surgery and believes that
it's imperative that the surgery be performed immediately. Otherwise, the patient might expire due to
heart failure.

In this instance, it's really a matter of life or
death. Either the patient can act to rectify the problem
or face a greater potential of dying. The patient has
to make a choice. What choice would you make? It
seems fairly obvious, but life choices aren't always
straightforward.

Most of us would probably choose to have surgery to extend our life. And, the good news is that God wants us to have a long, fruitful life. He doesn't want us to have heart failure. He doesn't want us to have a hardened heart. He wants us to have a heart of flesh, which He provides to us when we receive Him as Lord and Savior. (Ezek. 36:26) He wants us to have a loving, tender, gentle, and compassionate heart. (1 Pet. 3:8)

So, if you've already received Christ, then you already have that kind of heart. "For it is with your heart that you believe and are justified." (Rom. 10:10) But, knowing this, sometimes circumstances arise that chip away at us and negatively impact our heart. Different life situations can arise to cause stress, strain, sin, and pain. The result is a heart that becomes hardened by anger, bitterness, or some other troubling emotion, which leads to heartbreak. We then have a heart condition that needs surgery.

Fortunately for us, God is the Great Physician. He provides us rest. Rest to the weary, cleansing from sin, and healing of a broken heart. (Jer. 6:16; Job 3:17; Ps. 62:1) Once we receive His love, mercy, and grace, He restores our heart and makes it like His. He gives us a new heart, new spirit, removes any hardness, and gives us a heart of flesh. (Ezek. 36:26)

If you are suffering from a heart condition ask God to remove your heart and give you a new heart. It's your decision. Why not ask Him today?

Affirmation

Lord, Reshape My Heart:
- When I have been hurt by a loved one
- When I am being mistreated by others
- When I lose someone close in an accident
- When I am experiencing hardship and difficulty
- When I am rebounding from a broken relationship

Meditation Verse

"The Lord is my shepherd; I shall not be in want. He makes me lie down in green pastures, he leads beside quiet waters, he restores my soul. He guides me in paths of righteousness for his name's sake." (Ps. 23:1-2)

Discussion Questions

1. Think about a time when you suffered from a broken heart. How did you feel? How long did you have those feelings? Are you healed? If not, how will you get there? If so, how did you break free? Explain.

2. If you were a doctor how would you advise a patient who had a serious heart condition and needed surgery immediately? How would you approach the subject? What would you say to persuade the person to have the surgery?

3. Survey your heart. Do you need to have surgery? If so, what do you want God to remove? Fix? Be honest with yourself.

Prayer

Glorify the name of the Lord. I praise the name of the Lord. I cry out to you, oh God. Please Lord, change my heart. I know that the heart reflects the character of the man. And so I pray that the good that is in me would pour out as loving, kind, considerate, and generous. I am suffering from a heart condition. I need you to operate because I don't want to remain like I am. I desire a new heart. I want a fresh start. Give me rest from all the stress, strain, sin, and pain. I want to be like your son, Jesus. Amen.

Reflection

_____

_____

_____

_____

_____

Praise Your Name

"My mouth is filled with your praise,
declaring your splendor all day long."
(Psalm 71:8)

It's easy to praise God when things are going right. But, can you still praise Him when things in life seem to be out of control? Some challenges people face include incarceration, death of a loved one, a broken relationship, loss of a job, mistreatment by others, or some other kind of difficulty. The mountaintop moments are fantastic, but God wants you to continue to praise Him when you find yourself walking through what feels like the Valley of the Shadow of Death. (Ps. 23:4)

Consider these stories:

Paul and Silas were attacked, stripped, beaten, flogged, and imprisoned. (Acts 16: 22) While in prison, they sang praises to God while they were confined in prison. "About midnight [they] were praying and singing hymns to God and the other prisoners were listening to them." (Acts 16:25) Rather than wallow in self-pity based on their circumstances, they lifted up the Lord and offered Him praise. Then, the passage goes on to say that suddenly there was a great earthquake and the prison doors opened. (Acts 16:25-26)

The children of Israel had a lot of challenges prior to crossing the Jordan River and entering Gilgal as well. After arriving in Gilgal, the Lord spoke to

Joshua and told him that He had delivered Jericho into his hands. (Joshua 6:2) In obedience, Joshua and the children of Israel faithfully praised God by walking around the walls of Jericho, blowing their trumpets. (Joshua 6:12-16) Soon thereafter, there was a great shout and the walls crumbled before them. (Joshua 6:20)

Another example is when Jehoshaphat became aware the Moabites and Ammonites were planning to make war against him. In anticipation, he sent a praise team (members of his army) ahead and they praised God. "Jehoshaphat appointed men to sing to the Lord and to praise him for the splendor of his holiness as they went out at the head of the army." (2 Ch. 20:21) "As they began to sing and praise, the Lord set ambushes against their [enemies], and they were defeated." (2 Ch. 22) Through his obedience to God, Jehoshaphat experienced a great victory.

Are you experiencing turmoil? Are you feeling hurt, left out, or rejected? If so, then now's the time to lift your voice up to God. Put aside what you think and praise your Father in heaven. He can make a way out of no way. Praise Him all the way to victory and continue to declare His glory. "How good it is to sing praises to our God, how pleasant and fitting to praise him." (Ps. 147:1)

Affirmation

Father, praise your name:
- When I am trying to overcome an addiction
- Because you are the only one I can count on
- When my boss is mistreating me at work

- Because I recognize your undying love for me
- When is seems like nothing is going right in my life

Meditation Verse

"I will bow down toward your holy temple and will praise your name for your love and your faithfulness for you are exalted above all things, your name and your word." (Psa. 138)

Discussion Questions

1. Do you carve out time to give God praise other than Sunday morning? When? Where? How? Why should you praise Him?
2. Reflect on a difficult time in your life when you praised God despite your situation. How did praising Him help you? Are you experiencing difficulty right now? If so, should you praise Him? Will you?
3. Look up various psalms that refer to praising God. What patterns do you see? Any new insights? Spend time meditating on the passage(s) you read.

Prayer

Oh faithful Lord, I praise you. I praise all the angels and heavenly hosts. I praise the sun, moon, stars, and sky. I give praise for everything because it's all part of your creation. You set everything in place forever and ever. You gave decrees that will last forevermore. Let the name of the Lord be praised.

Your name alone shall be exalted. Your splendor is found on earth and in the heavens above. Praise the Lord. Amen.

Reflection

_____

_____

_____

_____

_____

RESTORE MY SOUL

"He makes me lie down in green pastures,
He leads me beside the quiet waters,
He restores my soul." (Psalm 23:2-3)

Busyness is a way of life in our society today. And, accompanying busyness is stress. Through cellular phones, computers, and email, our lives have become more productive, but more stressful too. As a result, we often experience more head-aches, sleep disorders, and other health-related prob-lems. Our body tells us to slow down, get some rest, take a vacation, etc. But, oftentimes, we ignore the warning signs and continue to travel down the road of busyness.

This might be a new revelation for some, but God is not the author of stress. He is the Good Shepherd who wants us to be still and find a place of peace for His name's sake. (Ps. 23:1) He doesn't want us to be fearful of anything because He is a Restorer. (Ps. 23:3) He doesn't want us to suffer in any way because he is a Comforter. (Ps. 23:4) God, the Omniscient One, desires for us to make time to stop and rest. He wants us to follow Him, to lie down in green pastures and lay beside quiet waters. (Ps. 23:2) In our obedience, He restores us physically, mentally, spiritually, and emotionally. And, His goodness and love follows us all the days of our life. (Ps. 23:6)

Are you too busy? Dealing with a lot of family-related issues? Working too many hours in a stressful work environment? Always on the telephone, sending text messages, emailing, or working on the computer? Are you trying to get ahead and losing sight of what's really important in life? If so, then perhaps this is message is for you.

If busyness has become a way of life for you and you know you need to make time for God, stop and embrace the rest He has for you. Follow the Lord all the days of your life and you will dwell in His house forever. (Ps. 23:6) "He will call upon me, and I will answer him." (Ps. 91:15)

Affirmation

Lord, Restore My Soul:
- As I wake up in the morning
- When I am preoccupied with work
- So my physical body can heal
- When I need to stop and focus on you
- So I can dwell with you forever

Meditation Verse

"And the God of all grace, who called you to his eternal glory in Christ, after you have suffered a little while, will himself restore you and make you strong, firm, and steadfast." (1 Pet. 5: 10)

Discussion Questions

1. In what area(s) of your life are you too busy? How can you make time to slow down? Do you need God to restore you?

2. Where do you go to find restoration? To the beach? A church? A private place? What do you do when you arrive there? Explain.

3. What does the Bible say about restoration of the soul? Take some time to meditate on several passages that you find helpful. Ask God to help you find a place to rest your soul.

Prayer

Lord, I feel weary, worn, tattered, and torn. I know I am way too busy. I feel like I can't get everything done in a day. I feel the pressure to work to get results. But I know that you don't see things the same way. If I trust you more I know you will give me more time. If I trust you more I know you will cause me to slow down. I know if I trust you more, I will slow down and realize that everything will be okay. Help me find rest and restore me so that I have the right perspective about life. After I suffer for a little while, you will make me strong. Thank you in advance for what you are going to do. In Jesus' mighty name. Amen.

Reflection

_____

_____

_____

_____

_____

ADJUST MY FOCUS

"The Lord does not look at the things man
looks at. Man looks at the outward
appearance, but the Lord looks at the heart."
(I Sam. 16:7)

Living in the world today is like being inside a pressure cooker. You must have a big house, a fancy car, and a job that pays a lot of money. You must wear the finest clothes and do whatever it takes to keep up with the next man. Some people have to keep up with Mr. Jones, our neighbor who seems to be doing better. The more he has, the more we want and we let societal pressures bring us to the boiling point where we are about to burst.

Your mistake in reason is that you believe that all these things really matter. They don't. What God is really concerned with is whether your heart is right. Do you possess good character? Are you a man of integrity? Those unseen qualities are really what matter to Him. Is your heart clean, without blemish or stain? Is your heart pure and totally committed to God? Are you doing what is pleasing in God's sight? After all, He is watching you.

If you answered, "no" to any of these questions, then you need to realize that God is not concerned with your accumulation of stuff or how you appear to others. Rather, He wants you to focus on making sure your heart is pure. He wants your life to be without blemish or stain. He desires that you be like His son, Jesus. This is how God sees you.

A good prayer to pray is the one David spoke after he fell short with Bathsheba. David said, "Create in me a pure heart, Oh God, and renew a steadfast spirit within me. Do not cast me from your presence or take Your Holy Spirit from me. Restore to me the joy of your salvation and grant me a willing spirit to sustain me." (Ps. 51:10-11) Have you asked the Master to help you adjust your focus?

Affirmation

Father, help me Adjust My Focus when:
- I have difficulty getting along with people
- I feel tempted to lust with my eyes
- I find myself being judgmental toward others
- I experience someone who is different from me
- I receive correction or rebuke at church

Meditation Verse

"I know, Oh Lord, that a man's life is not his own; it is not for man to direct his steps. Correct me, Lord, but only with justice." (Jer. 10:23, 24)

Discussion Questions

1. Read Psalm 51. What did David do to help readjust his focus? How did his focus become unaligned with God's plan for him?
2. What tactics does the enemy use to try to keep us focused away from the things God has for

us? Are there helpful biblical passages that reveal these tactics?

3. Is your heart right with the Lord? Is everything okay with your soul? Are you putting God first in all areas of your life? Is he truly Lord over every area of your life? Be honest with yourself.

Prayer

Father, I come before Thee asking that you hear my prayer. May it not fall on deaf ears. I come asking with a pure heart for you to change me from the inside out. I can no longer live in this raggedy body without making you my top priority. I pray that you would renew my heart and put a steadfast spirit in me. Let me kneel in your presence because a drop of your goodness gives me everything I need. Father, I love you so much. I pray that you would hear this prayer. In Jesus' name. Amen.

Reflection

_____

_____

_____

_____

_____

LET MY WORDS BE YOURS

"He who guards his mouth and his tongue
keeps himself from calamity."
(Proverbs 21:23)

Do you remember when you told your first lie? Many people told their first lie as a child. You told your mother, "I didn't take any cookies from the cookie jar." Meanwhile, she is looking at you with crumbs on our face and a half eaten cookie hidden in your hand. We didn't know better so we tried to cover up our wrongdoing.

Many people stopped lying once they knew better. But, some of us, even as adults, still tell lies today. Some try to keep secrets from their spouse to cover hidden sin. Some lie to get ahead at work or to elevate themselves in the eyes of others. Some lie to inflate credentials, to inflate ego, to get over, to get ahead, or simply because of ignorance.

Some of the most influential people in the world have lied. Is there a world leader, politician, business man, professional athlete, music star, or other person whom you know has lied? We all know someone who has lied. But, why do you choose to carry such a heavy burden? Lying seems easy, but the weight you carry because of it is extremely heavy. And, one lie flows from another until you reach the point when you can't even remember the truth.

Fortunately, the God of all truth tells us to "keep your tongue from evil and your lips from speaking lies (Ps. 34:13 with I Pet. 3:100) because He knows that this will only lend to calamity and your own self destruction. The alternative is to say, "God let your words flow from my mouth." Help me guard my mouth and tongue so that the only words I speak are those that glorify you.

Affirmation

Master, Let My Words Be Yours:
- In the workplace and at home
- When I am tempted to tell a lie
- To guide my mouth and tongue
- So I would glorify your name
- Because it's your desire that I be truthful

Meditation Verse

"Set an example for the believers in speech, in life, in love, in faith, and in purity." (1 Tim. 4:12)

Discussion Questions

1. Do you remember when a public figure or official lied about something? How did it make you feel when that person lied? Did it change how you looked at that person? Did it affect how you live? Explain.

2. What does the Bible say about the tongue and lying lips? How do you apply the principles you've learned to your life? How can you make truthfulness a permanent habit?

3. Are there circumstances where you believe it's appropriate to tell a lie? If so, when and why? Explain.

Prayer

Father, I confess. I don't always make the right decisions or do the right thing. But, I am a work in progress and I desire to walk down the straight path that you have laid for me. I do not desire to curse or use inappropriate language. I do not desire to tell course jokes or offend Thee with my mouth in any way. Help me reign in my tongue such that my words will only lift you up. May you be glorified through my mouth. In Jesus' name. Amen.

Reflection

_____

_____

_____

_____

_____

YOU SHALL SUPPLY ALL MY NEEDS

"And my God will meet all your needs
according to his glorious riches in Christ
Jesus." (Phil. 4:19)

Do you remember when you were an infant? Most of us probably don't have any memories from when we were just entering the world. It was a time when we were essentially helpless. We needed someone (mom, dad, grandma, grandpa, or someone else) to help us with almost everything. You had to be fed by someone because you couldn't feed yourself, and, of course, you didn't know how to cook, but you had to eat. You had someone change your diaper because you couldn't do it yourself. You had someone hold and caress you when you felt discomfort because you did not know how to comfort yourself. You had someone help you with your needs because you were just a baby.

But, the reality is that while your family could take care of some of your needs, they couldn't provide everything. For instance, if you became ill, your mother would take you to the doctor. The doctor would evaluate the problem and then prescribe medication or take some other course of action to help you return to good health. Sometimes we need a specialist to help us with our needs. A specialist can care for matters like no one else can. However, a specialist has limitations. A specialist (i.e. doctor) works well in his field of study, but he cannot help you in other disciplines (i.e., car repairs).

God is like those people in our life who care for us. He loves you, cares for you, and desires to care for your needs. But, unlike humans, he doesn't provide for just one area of need. He provides for all of your needs based on your relationship with His son Jesus Christ. He meets your emotional, physical, financial, and relational needs. He meets you right where you are in more ways than you can imagine. God simply wants you to trust Him. He wants you to know that He is God. He wants you to ask Him to meet all of your needs. And, if you do, "He will do exceeding, abundantly above and beyond that which [you] can ask, think or imagine." (Eph. 4:20)

Have you asked God to supply all of your needs? The Bible says that you can cast every care and concern upon the Lord. (Ps. 55:22) Have you turned to Him and asked, "Lord, please take these burdens of mine? If not, isn't now a good time?

Affirmation

Lord, I know You Supply All My Needs:
- When I am having difficulty with my supervisor
- So I can overcome my sickness
- When I find parenting overwhelming
- In moments when I am tempted to sin
- Because you are the Only One who can

Meditation Verse

"The Lord will guide you always; he will satisfy your needs in a sun-scorched land and will strengthen your frame. You will be a well-watered garden, like a spring whose waters never fail." (Isa. 58:11)

Discussion Questions

1. What is your greatest need? Have you ever thought about it? What is it? Have you asked God to help you with it? Have you shared it with anyone?

2. Do you think it is okay to pray about your own personal needs? Why or why not? Why should we ask God to help us with our needs? Doesn't he already know? If we should ask Him, how should we speak to Him?

3. What kind of needs does God help us with? Is there biblical evidence to support your answer? List the relevant passages and then schedule some time for meditation.

Prayer

Father, you tell me in your Word that I can come before you and cast every care and concern on you. I do so willingly and humbling myself before you. I pray that you would meet me right where I am. I know that you are the Great Provider and so I ask that you would provide for me and my family. You provide materials things, but you richly provide that which is unseen – integrity, character, self-discipline, self-control, and much more. God, meet me where I am right now. I desperately need you. In Jesus' name. Amen.

Reflection

_____

_____

_____

_____

_____

HELP ME DO GOOD

"If your enemy is hungry, feed him; if he is
thirsty give him something to drink.
In doing this, you will heap burning coals on
his head." (Romans 12:20)

When someone hurts you the natural human tendency is to want to get back at them. You might want to say some hurtful words. You might want to talk behind their back. You might want to act out in some way to let them know how much you were hurt or offended. You really want that person to know exactly what it felt like when they hurt you. So, many of us will use hurtful words, hit, smack, punch, kick, or lash out in other hurtful ways against others.

For a Christian man, these actions beg the question, "What would Jesus do?" That is the question every man must answer. Although, at the time it seems like it makes sense to lash out and avenge those who hurt us, the reality is that's not how Jesus would respond. Responding with threats, burst of anger, shouting, or other negative behavior makes you only susceptible to darkness. The Bible says God is light; in him there is no darkness at all. If we claim to have fellowship with him...we [must] walk in the light." (1 John 1:5-7) In other words, even when we encounter our enemies, we must walk in a spirit of love like Jesus.

Why? Love conquers all. Jesus knew the power of a loving response. (John 8) He even looked specific offenses right in the eye because He knew that a loving response would truly bless His enemy. (Ibid) As an imitator of Christ, you are called to be a blessing to your enemy too. Your loving response can leave them not knowing what to do and can bless others too. Your enemies expect one thing and get the exact opposite. It's God's goodness that leads them to repentance. You're loving words or action might be the very thing that leads someone to a personal relationship with Jesus Christ.

Affirmation

Lord, Help Me Do Good:
- To win souls into the kingdom
- At home, work, and in the community
- Because you've called me to love my enemies
- When I am tempted to be hurtful to others
- So I can be a blessing to you

Meditation Verse

"Let us not become weary in doing good, for at the proper time we will reap a harvest if we do not give up. Therefore, as we have opportunity, let us do good to all people...." (Gal. 6:9-10)

Discussion Questions

1. Why does God want you to do good deeds? Can you articulate several reasons? What kinds of things should you be doing before you die?

2. Do you know how to love your enemies? Talk about an experience when you loved an enemy. Is there someone in your life now you are having difficulty loving? Explain.

3. Have you talked to God about dealing with unlovable people? Spend some time in prayer and speak honestly to God about this area of your life.

Prayer

Abba Father, your Word says that a righteous man will have many troubles, but the Lord will take care of them all. And, I pray that you will help me with those who are determined to come against me; those standing in my way; those trying to cause my heart to become bitter. It's hard to pray for my enemies, but I know that you want me to so that I set them before you and allow you to soften their heart. I pray for a miracle and trust that you would workout everything for your glory. I pray also that you would work in me too. Mold me in such a way that my enemies see a change in me causing them to change because of the light coming from me. Oh God, I leave everything in your hands. In Jesus' name. Amen.

Reflection

_____

_____

_____

_____

_____

THANK YOU LORD

"You turned my wailing into dancing; you
removed my sackcloth
and clothed me with joy that my heart may
sing to you and not be silent.
O Lord, my God, I will give you thanks
forever. (Psalm 30:11-12)

Many people don't stop often enough and give thanks to God for what He has done. We get so busy with work, family, hobbies, projects, and the busyness of life that we lose sight of why everything we do is possible. Saying, "Thank you," communicates our appreciation to our Great Provider. This is one of the first lessons you learn as a child. Evan, say, "Thank you," son.

You must stop and say, "Thank you Lord for all you have done in my life and for the many blessings you continue to bestow upon me. Thank you for my job, marriage, kids, car, house, pets, friends, etc. Lord, thank you for safe travel, job promotion, helping me to finish school, getting married, having children, and so much more." Don't worry about what you don't have. Thank God for what you do have. "Therefore, since we are receiving a kingdom that cannot be shaken, let us be thankful, and so worship God acceptably with reverence and awe." (Heb. 12:28) When you look at things with the right perspective, it will change how you see the world.

When you express your thankfulness to God, you also say, "I trust you." I trust you as Lord over every area of my life. I trust you for my waking up and my lying down. I trust you morning, noon, and night." If you have a specific prayer request, make time to thank God in advance for providing for that need. We ought to give thanks in anticipation of God blessing us. God will fulfill our needs because He has promised to do so. "God will meet all of your needs according to his glorious riches in Christ Jesus." (Phil. 4:19) Pray this prayer: "Thank you Father for everything you've done for me in the past, present and future. I trust that you will be true to your Word and fulfill all of your promises. Again, I say, Thank you! In Jesus' name. Amen.

Affirmation

I say, Thank You Lord:
- For getting me out of a difficult situation
- In anticipation of you meeting my needs
- Because you are a Great Provider
- For helping me get through my depression
- While I am going through a difficult season

Meditation Verse

"The Lord protects the simple hearted; when I was in great need, he saved me." (Ps. 116: 6)

Discussion Questions

1. When is the last time you thanked God for all he has done for you? If you haven't lately,

what's wrong with right now? Stop and thank Him for the many blessings in your life.

2. What does it mean to be thankful to God? How do you express your thankfulness to Him? Do you thank Him when things are going well? Explain.
3. How would you go about establishing a habit of thanking God everyday? What are some good practices you can put into place immediately? Discuss.

Prayer

I come to say thank you Lord for all you've done for me in the past. I praise your name because you are worthy of all praise. I honor you because you are worthy of all honor. You are the Alpha and Omega, the First and the Last, the Beginning and the End. You are a great and awesome God. You are Jehovah Jireh my provider. You provide for all of my needs. I pray that you would watch over me. Guide me, mold me, shape me, and hold me. I will praise your name at all times. In Jesus' name. Amen."

Reflection

_____

_____

_____

_____

_____

TAKE ME HIGHER

"As the heavens are higher than the earth, so
are my ways higher than your ways and my
thoughts than your thoughts. (Isa. 55:9)

Have you ever worked in an office where you noticed co-workers stepping on each other to get ahead? Do you remember your school days when your peers competed to get the best grades? Human reasoning is rather interesting because we believe what we think is true. If I execute my plans just so, then the fruit of my labor will be successful and I will achieve my goal. Well, our human reasoning may seem to us to be the right way to look at things in life, but God's ways are the exact opposite of ours.

Jesus said that many who are first shall be last, and the last shall be first. (Mark 10:31). What did this mean? Well, Jesus' words were a warning against pride in regard to personal accomplishments because we cannot accomplish our end goals on our own. "With man this is impossible, but not with God, all things are possible with God." (Mark 10:27) Man says we earn our salvation, but God says it is a gift that is freely given. When we allow our reasoning to enter the equation of our success, assuming we had something to do with it, we miss the lesson that Jesus sought to teach.

This is why it's so important to learn to listen and hear God's voice. God is speaking all the time. The question is: Are you listening? The Bible says, "For my thoughts are not your thoughts, neither are your ways my ways, declares the Lord." (Isa. 55:8) God's thoughts are different from ours. God's ways are different from our ways. When we get more in tune with our heavenly Father, He allows our thoughts and ways to become more like His.

If you live according to man's ways, then you will reap only earthly results. However, if you live according to God's ways, then the implications are eternal and everlasting. Are you at a place in life where the focus is about you and your dreams? Have your considered God's dreams for you? Perhaps, you have been working toward some goal in life, but haven't achieved the results you wanted. Or, you've achieved some goal, but still feel emptiness. Well, in either case, the answer is very clear. Give God a try. He can fill in what's missing. He wants to take you higher. He has an even better outcome awaiting you. Why don't you give Him all your thoughts and ways today? Ask Him to take you higher. You will be glad you did.

Affirmation
Lord, Take Me Higher:
- So I can be the best husband
- In raising my children
- In my quest to be an authentic man of God
- In all of my professional endeavors
- So I can be more like you

Meditation Verse

"I will ascend above the tops of the clouds; I will make myself like the Most High." (Isa. 14:14)

Discussion Questions

1. Read Isaiah 55:8-9 to yourself. How do you interpret the passage? In what area(s) of your life do you think on your own? How can you allow your thoughts and ways to be displaced by God's thoughts and ways?
2. Reflect on work, school, or other experience where you relied on your own thoughts and ways and did not reach your goal. How did the experience make you feel? What could you have done differently?
3. Read Romans 12:2. How do you fully commit to God's agenda for our life?

Prayer

God you created the heavens and earth and all that dwells in it. I cannot fathom how great your love is for me. You have given me breath to wake up everyday. I praise your name. For you have called me to righteousness and I will take hold of your hand and not let go. Open my eyes that I might consider you everyday. I want to go higher in your glory. I want all you have for me. As I decrease in the things of me, I pray that I would increase in the things of you. This is your humble servant's prayer. In Jesus' name. Amen.

Reflection

_____

_____

_____

_____

ALL THINGS WORK TOGETHER

"All things God works for the good of
those who love him, who have been called
according to purpose." Romans 8:28

Have you ever asked the question, "Why do bad things happen to good people?" It's a question that we struggle to find the answer to. And, rarely, if ever, do we find an answer. Perhaps, you've known someone who died in a car accident or had a friend suffer from a serious illness. Perhaps, you've known someone who is regularly hospitalized or someone who has experienced some other tragedy. Perhaps, that person is you. No matter the case, the reality is that bad things do happen to good people. The list includes friends, family, co-workers, school class-mates, etc. The loss of anyone is tragic. But, when it's a good person, it seems to be especially painful. So how should you deal with the pain and hurt when you deal with losing someone?

Well, you have several options. First, you could ask, "Why, why, why?" You can question God and ask him to tell you why the situation occurred. But, many times you either don't get an answer that helps you fully understand or it takes a lot longer than you expect. Second, you could simply spend your days mourning and feeling blue. While mourning is okay for a while, it's not healthy to stay stuck because then you can't move forward. Third, you could specula-tively formulate various theories why the incident occurred, but that really doesn't help. This approach doesn't allow you to gain any ground. And, oftentimes, it only opens the door to more unanswered questions.

So, what should you do? The answer is to trust God. He is the Creator of all things. (Gen. 1-2) He is the Answer to all of our questions. As the great preacher, Charles Stanley, says, "God uses everything as a tool for His glory." God allows certain things to happen in life that are outside of our control. He allows bad things to happen to good people to fulfill His will here on earth. God works everything together like a nice stew because in the end He knows the outcome will be magnificent. He works according to His purpose and plan – all of which has not been revealed to His children. All we need to know is that he works everything together – good and bad – of those who love Him, and who know Him as Lord. (Rom. 8:28)

Affirmation

Father, All Things Work Together:
- When I am confronted by a tragic situation
- For my friend who died in an auto accident
- In times of hardship, struggle and despair
- For my loved one who is ill in the hospital
- When I or someone I know has cancer

Meditation Verse

"Now we know that if the earthly tent we live in is destroyed, we have a building from God, an

eternal house in heaven, not built by human hands."
(2 Cor. 5:1)

Discussion Questions

1. Why do you suppose God allows suffering? How do we find God in our suffering? How does He use suffering to fulfill His purposes?

2. Do you know of a good person that something bad has happened to? Explain.

3. How can you come alongside someone suffering? How can you minister to someone in difficult circumstances? Share with someone or in a small group.

Prayer

Lord, I do not always come to you knowing how to pray. And, a special uncertainty comes around times of loss. I don't always know what to say, but I do have a lot of questions. This particular situation is in your hands. I realize you know far more than me, not just a little bit more. So, I rest in the fact that you are God. Let your will be done on earth as it is in heaven. Father, I would ask that you help me with the things I don't understand. Help me make peace with the unknown. I don't have all the answers. I may never have all the answers, but surely peace can find me if I seek her. I rest in your arms, loving father. This is the prayer of your servant. Bless your name. Amen.

Reflection

_____

_____

_____

_____

_____

RUNNING FOR A REASON

"Do you not know that in a race all the
runners run, but only one gets the prize?
Run in such a way as to get the prize."
(I Corinthians 9:4)

Have you ever run in a race or watched someone compete? Well, if so, then you realize that there are a few important components to running a good race.

First, a runner must have a good start. A sprinter has to get out of the blocks as quickly as possible in order to gain an advantage over the competition.

Second, a runner must run at a steady pace throughout the race in order to finish first. A long distance runner must pace himself until the finish line is in sight.

Third, and finally, a runner must have a strong finish. Finishing well is important for any runner about to cross the finish line. A runner must not only run to the finish line, but through it as well to assure that no one else gains the final advantage. The runner who does each of these things the best will most likely be the top finisher who receives the prize.

God wants you to take the same approach in your everyday walk with him. You make a good start everyday by regularly reading your Bible and giving thanks to the Lord through prayer. If you start off on the right foot, then you put yourself in position to discover what God wants from you.

Throughout our life journey, we must also train and build up our spiritual muscles so we can become a mature believer. The Bible says, that everyone who competes in the games goes into strict training (I Cor. 9:25). We grow by practicing good spiritual habits everyday. "Not running like a man aimlessly or beating the air (I Cor. 9:26)." The second component is joining together in regular fellowship, Bible study, and accountability with others so you're progressively sanctified.

And everyday must not only be a focus on simply running the race, but also on finishing well because "only one gets the prize." (1 Cor. 9: 27) God doesn't want you to give up. "Men always ought to pray and not lose heart." (Luke18:1) He wants you to cross the finish line to the cheers of the angels in heaven.

Therefore, you ought to maximize the gifts God has given you because tomorrow is not promised for anyone. You ought to make the most of every opportunity and run in such a way as to win the race, (I Cor. 9:24), lest you be disqualified for the prize. (1 Cor. 9:27)

Are you running a good race? Do you start well in the morning? Are you growing and maturing in the things of God? Are you running through the finish line and finishing well? If you answered any of these questions negatively, then, perhaps, you need to refocus so you can get back on track.

Affirmation
Lord, I am Running For A Reason:
- When I have fallen away from trusting you

- Because of the outpouring of your love for me
- When my spiritual gas tank feels like it's empty
- To help me understand who I am as child of God
- Because I want to hear you say, "Well done"

Meditation Verse

"Be diligent in these matters; give yourself wholly to them, so that everyone may see your progress." 1 Tim. 4:15

Discussion Questions

1. Take a moment and evaluate your life. In what areas do you believe you are under performing? What area(s) are you not giving God your best? What do you need to do to improve?

2. What do you do on a daily, weekly, or monthly basis to grow and mature as a Christian believer? Do you think you are doing enough? If not, what more should you do?

3. Who else is involved in helping you grow spiritually? Are you accountable to someone? Do you fellowship regularly with others? What would a friend or family member say about your spiritual walk with Christ?

Prayer

Oh God, I want to run well for you. I want to run a strong race and finish well. I know that you have a purpose for my life so I am running for a reason. I seek to attain to the higher calling you have for me in Christ Jesus. I run because of your love and kindness toward me. I run because you've spared me another day. I run because you are so very faithful. I pray that I'd be diligent in all matters that pertain to you so that everyone would see my progress and I would be approved in your sight. In Jesus' name. Amen.

Reflection

_____

_____

_____

_____

_____

GIVE ME A GENEROUS HEART

"You will be made rich in everyway so that
you can be generous on every occasion,
and through us your generosity will result in
thanksgiving to God." (2 Cor. 9:11)

Have you ever met a stingy person? Stingy
people aren't fun to be around. They never want to
share anything. They always want to keep everything
to themselves. Mine. Mine. Mine. Some folks are
so stingy that they even hoard their excesses. They
could come into a million dollars yet still share very
little with others. Stingy people think it's all about
them. Like a little child they want to play with all
the toys and not let anyone participate. Stingy people
have the wrong attitude about life.

Fortunately for us God is not stingy. Could you
imagine if he was? In his sovereignty, he could simply
cut off his mercy and grace. And then we'd really be
in a heap of trouble. What if God decided to cut off
your air supply because He wanted to breathe all the
air for himself? What would you do then? Well, the
honest answer is there's not much you could do but
die.

But, thankfully, God is always generous. He is
generous on every occasion and never stops. No
matter how much we might try, we could never be
more generous than Him. You can't out give God!
However, if we model ourselves after His son and
practice generosity everyday, then He promises to

bless us. "A generous man will himself be blessed, for he shares his food with the poor." (Prov. 22:9) God wants us to "put [our] hope in [Him], who richly provides us with everything for our enjoyment." (1 Tim. 6:17) His desire is that we'd be "rich in good deeds, and to be generous and willing to share." (1 Tim. 6:19)

Do you consider yourself a generous person? What would others say about you? If you could be more generous to others how would you make that change? Will you allow your heart to be a reflection of God in the area of giving?

Affirmation

Oh God, Give Me a Generous Heart:
- When I am disinclined to share with others
- With my time, talent, and treasure
- As I spend time with family and friends
- That I might be more than a 10% tither
- So my heart will be pure like yours

Meditation Verse

"Good will come to him who is generous." (Psalm 112:5)

Discussion Questions

1. Sharing food, lending money, and defending rights are ways that we can show kindness. What other things can a person do to show generosity to others?
2. What kinds of things do you do that you believe are generous acts? Does the Bible

provide examples of generous acts? Give several examples and explain.

3. When you are generous what do you get in return? Should you expect to get something in return for your generosity? How can a person learn to be more generous?

Prayer

Father, I pray that you'd allow me to have a giving heart. Whether I am already a generous person or a stingy one, I pray that you would expand the range of my heart. I want to be one who gives to others freely, without any expectation of receiving in return. I don't want to give grudgingly or with the wrong attitude. Lord, I want to be filled with a loving spirit that would give because that's what you want me to do. I pray that you would change me right now. In Jesus' name. Amen.

Reflection

_____

_____

_____

_____

_____

LOOKING THROUGH YOUR EYES

"The Lord does not look at the things man
looks at. Man looks at the outward appearance, but the Lord looks at the heart."
(I Sam. 16:7)

Have you heard the phrase, "Don't judge a book
by its cover?" You probably have heard that saying
growing up. The words represent an invaluable phrase
that people unfortunately violate everyday. Bias,
prejudice, discrimination are some of the primary
offenders. But, people also make judgments about
one another everyday based on skin color, ethnicity,
rational origin, weight, height, intelligence, etc.

This is what it means to be a human being. It's
human nature. People make judgments based upon
ignorance or not fully appreciating differences. Some
make judgments based upon lack of information or
a quick assessment of someone based on something
assumed. Our human nature has a way of getting
in the way of some of the good things we could be
doing. If only we could get 'our nature' out of the
way.

Think about how difficult it is when someone
judges you. You feel isolated, excluded, left out, or
left behind. Perhaps, you felt that way as a young
person when others didn't want to be your friend
because you looked a certain way or you weren't part
of the in crowd for some reason. It's painful feeling
this way as a child. But, it can be equally disturbing

as an adult. You can experience these same kind of behaviors in the workplace, school, with friends and family, etc. It doesn't matter where it happens it's often pretty painful. You might be able to keep up a good appearance on the outside, but on the inside you are really hurting.

Fortunately, God doesn't judge like man. He doesn't judge based upon one's outward appearance. Rather, he judges based upon what's inside one's heart. (1 Sam. 16:7) So, if you adopt the right heart, God's heart, about how you look at others, then you can have confidence of the Day of Judgment that God will smile upon you. This confidence can only come when you see things through God's eyes. "Therefore, let us stop passing judgment." (Rom. 14:13) Through God's eyes, you can see differently. Through His eyes you exercise sound judgment.

Affirmation

Lord, Looking Through Your Eyes:
- I don't judge others through ignorance
- I don't discriminate against others
- I won't be tempted to be judgmental
- I remain confident when others judge me
- I am worthy of being called a son of God

Meditation Verse

"I pray also that the eyes of your heart may be enlightened in order that you may know the hope to which he has called you...." (Ephesians 1:18)

Discussion Questions

1. Have you ever been discriminated against? Describe the situation and how it made you feel? Did you feel hurt? Offended? If so, how did you get your self and your emotions back on the right track?

2. What does the Bible say about judging others? Select a few passages and share your findings with a partner or in a small group. Why is it important not to judge others?

3. How does someone learn to stop judging others? Are we all guilty of judgment in one way or another? Can someone get delivered from being judgmental?

Prayer

Father, from you comes deliverance. You will not hold back your love from me. For I delight in your deliverance. You will deliver men whose ways are truthful. You will deliver men whose ways are right. You will deliver men whose ways are pure and holy. Lord, I surrender all of who I am to you. I pray that you would answer me as I call. Grant me a pure heart like yours. In Jesus name. Amen.

Reflection

_____

_____

_____

_____

_____

SEIZE THE MOMENT

"So be careful how you live. Don't live like
fools, but like those who are wise. Make
the most of every opportunity in these evil
days." (Ephesians 5:15-16)

Every moment you are alive is an opportunity.
You can do your best in school to get good grades.
You can work hard at your place of employment for a
raise, bonus, or promotion. You can serve as a loving
parent to raise a respectful child. You can eat right
and work to maintain good health. You can simply
smile at someone or say, "Hello," and brighten someone's day. If you take care in how you live, you can
have a great life. It's all about taking advantage of
every opportunity.

The same principle is true for your spiritual life.
You can have a regular pray life and draw nearer to
God. You can dig deep into Scripture and experience
God revealing Himself to you. You can attend church
regularly, listen to the sermon message, and allow
God to minister to you heart. You can select regular
scripture verses to meditate on and let God renew
your mind. If you follow all of God's commands and
do what the Word says, you can have a wonderful
journey with the Lord. But, you have to take advantage of every opportunity.

What are you doing with the time God has given
you? Are you reading the Bible and praying regularly? Where do you spend most of your time? Are the

majority of your hours at work? Church? Elsewhere? If you asked God what he thought about you today, what would He say? Would He say, "My son (<u>fill in your name</u>) is seizing the moment?" If not, then your opportunity is here, right now!

Affirmation

God, help me Seize the Moment when:
- I am tempted to do evil
- I rob time from you at work
- I experience discouragement from others
- I have to work with unbelievers
- I know it glorifies you

Meditation Verse

"Do not merely listen to the word, and so deceive yourselves. Do what it says." (James 1:22)

Discussion Questions

1. How much time do you spend reading the Bible? Praying? Meditating? Fasting? At church? At work? Does your time reflect your priorities? Explain.

2. Do you make the most of your opportunities everyday? Why or why not? If not, what do you need to change to see improvement?

3. Have you ever shared the gospel message with someone? If not, when will you take advantage of the opportunity? God wants you to seize every moment because tomorrow is not promised.

Prayer

Father, you are magnificent. Every minute, day, and hour is on loan from you. You created time and I ought to glorify you every waking moment of my life. I promise to take advantage of my time to do good, glorify you, encourage others, and work in such a way that others would come to know you as Lord and Savior. I thank you in advance for what you are going to do and how you will use me. I pray to remain obedient to your Word. I love you Lord. In Jesus' name I pray. Amen.

Reflection

_____

_____

_____

_____

_____

A Day Of New Beginnings

"I tell you the truth, no one can see the
Kingdom of God unless he is born again."
(John 3:3)

One reason why many men fail to accomplish
specific goals in life is due to their failure to get
started. You can think of a lot of great ideas, but if
you fail to take the necessary steps to carry out the
plan, then what good was the idea in the first place?
If you fail to execute the action items on our agenda
you won't reach your goal. However, if you considered everyday as a new beginning or a fresh start,
then, perhaps, you could avoid what might've been
and what possibly could've happened, and rather
be looking at what can be or what is. Even though
you cannot always go back and make a brand new
start, you can start from wherever you are right now
and make a brand new start. If you looked at things
through this lens, then everyday would have a brand
new beginning that would allow you to change course
and move in a new direction.

The same principle applies in our Christian life.
Today, can be a new day of no more lying, cheating,
stealing, adultery, lust, and other sin that offends
God. You cannot go back and change the past, you
cannot undue the past, but you can start fresh today.
You do this by asking God to forgive you of all of
your sin. "[E]veryone who believes in him receives
forgiveness of sins through his name." (Acts 10:43)

God offers you forgiveness from sin if you ask Him. "Ask and it will be given to you; seek and you will find; knock and the door will be opened to you." (Matt. 7:8) Once you ask, with a genuine heart, you are forgiven. Then, you are positioned to make a fresh start. "Who can forgive sins but God alone? (Mk. 2:7; Lk. 5:21)

If you are tired of carrying the heavy weight of your past, you can start afresh by rededicating your life right now. Ask him whatever you wish and it will be given to you. If you know that you've never had a relationship with the Lord, then today is your day too. You can have a personal relationship with Jesus Christ. To do so, you must be born again. This means you must: 1) accept Jesus into your heart; 2) believe that He died on the cross for your sins; and 3) confess Him as Lord of your life. Today is your day of new beginnings!

Affirmation

A Day of New Beginnings:
- When I feel angry, overwhelmed, stressed
- So I can leave my past hurts behind me
- So I can experience God's power in my life
- So I can have a relationship with you
- When I am feeling lonely and disconnected

Meditation Verse

"He put a new song in my mouth." (Ps. 40:3)

Discussion Questions

1. Do you have a relationship with God? Do you desire a relationship with Him? If so, would you like to accept His invitation of salvation by faith in Jesus Christ? Share with someone or in a small group.

2. Have you been living outside of God's will? Are you looking to make a fresh start? If so, won't you rededicate your life to Christ today? Share with someone or in a small group.

3. Are you feeling angry? Experiencing past hurt? Feeling lonely? Desiring to experience God's power? The only way to make a fresh start is to turn everything over to Jesus Christ. Isn't it time you did?

Prayer

God, I need a new beginning. I have tried things my way, but nothing has worked. I now want to give you a try. I confess the sins of my past and I am ready to move forward. I am tired of going through life sinking as if I am in quicksand. I need the traction that only you can give. I pray that you'd restore me through your love. In Jesus' name. Amen.

Reflection

_____

_____

_____

_____

_____

You Are My Hope

"Why so downcast, O my soul? Why so
disturbed within me? Put your hope in God,
for I will yet praise Him, my Savior.
(Psalm 42:5)

Have you ever seen someone who is hopeless?
Someone who is feeling blue? Depressed? Someone
who has given up on life? Suicidal? It's not a pretty
picture when all hope has seemingly run away. You
can see hopelessness on the face of people all around
the world today. People facing hunger, poverty, and
all sorts of despair. People confronted by job loss,
death of a loved one, and other crisis situations.
Many faced with dire circumstances with nothing or
no one to turn to.

Perhaps, you see hopelessness in the reflection
in the mirror when you wake up in the morning.
Perhaps, you are the one who is barely hanging onto
hope. Perhaps, you are encountering difficulties in
life right now and you feel as if no one is there for
you. Perhaps, you've been contemplating 'ending
it all' because your situation has made you so very
weary. You don't feel like looking forward to see if
hope is even there. You are empty, confused, feeling
trapped with no where else to go?

Well, if this sounds like you, then be encouraged
because there is One who brings and restores hope
when you think hope is lost. The One and Only One
that never goes away. God is the Source of all hope

and the hope for every man. My hope comes from God. (Ps. 62:5) You cannot do anything to muster up true hope for yourself. But, the Bible says, "[I]n his word have I put my hope." For the hope that is seen is really not hope at all. (Rom. 8:24) But, when you put your hope in the right place, "there is surely a future hope for you." (Ps. 23:18)

So, be reminded, even when circumstances are looking bleak, you can always trust God to bring you through. Hope from the Lord is not fleeting, it never goes away and it's always available. You have to trust God. He is the One through whom all hope must come. O Israel, put your hope in the Lord." (Ps. 130:7)

Affirmation
You Are My Hope when:
- There appears to be no other way out
- I feel depressed and empty inside
- My circumstances are overwhelming
- I am struggling with chemical dependency
- Everything appears to be lost

Meditation Verse
Remember, you are excluded…without hope and without God in the world. "But, now in Christ Jesus you who once were far away have been brought near through the blood of Christ." (Eph. 2:12-13)

Discussion Questions
1. Has there ever been a time in your life when you felt hopeless and you did not know

where to turn? What did you do? How did you respond?

2. Think about someone you know who was or is hopeless. How did they deal with their situation? Negatively? Positively? What did you learn from them?

3. Take some time to meditate on Isaiah 29:11. What does that verse say about hope? How does that verse encourage you to keep moving forward in your life?

Prayer

Thank you Lord that I can put all of my trust in you. The things I hope for I hope for through you. You always encourage my heart when I feel down. You pick me up when the sky outside is gray. You put a smile on my face when things just don't seem to be going my way. Lord, when nothing else is left I know that there's still hope because you promise me hope and a good future. I trust you at your Word. Thank you and bless your name. In Jesus' name. Amen.

Reflection

_____

_____

_____

_____

_____

SHINE YOUR FACE UPON ME

"The Lord bless you and keep you. The Lord
makes His face shine upon you,
and be gracious to you." (Numbers 6:24-26)

Have you ever noticed how good it feels when
someone smiles at you? Maybe it was getting a good
grade in school and your teacher smiled. Maybe
you won a race and your coach smiled. Maybe you
brought home a good grade and your parents smiled.
You did something great and a family member or
friend smiled. The smile was delightful and warmed
your heart. You already felt good, but the smile made
you feel even better. It feels so good when we experience someone smiling at us because it makes us
happy and causes us to smile even more.

God wants you to feel the same way when you
look at Him. He wants you to know that He is smiling
at you because you've done well in school, won a
race, or did something remarkable that made Him
smile. He smiles when you read His Word. He smiles
when you are on your knees praying to Him. He
smiles when you worship Him at church. He smiles
when you are living according to His purpose and
plan for your life. God smiles upon each man when
he does what God expects him to do.

The world today can be very cold. With job
losses, housing foreclosures, family and personal
issues, and all the challenges we experience today,
there are a lot of reasons not to smile. When you're

grieving the loss of a loved one or experiencing a broken dating or marital relationship, the world can seem pretty unfair. And, after a while, things in the world can seem very cold.

But, God's smile always makes us warm. His nature is filled with love. His presence is blessing. His very being consoles. And, the marvelous thing is He is already smiling at you. He is looking at each one of us with a smile that says, "Well done my son." He is truly a loving Father waiting to share the warmth of His glory. Did you know that the Son is shining His face upon you all the time? He wants you to know that He loves you and wants to let you know. Let His smile light up your life today, right now!

Affirmation
Lord, Shine Your Face Upon Me:
- So I can know the love of a father
- So I can feel the warmth of your presence
- So I can come out of my state of depression
- So I can be a shining light to warm others
- So I can shine 100 times brighter

Meditation Verse
"The Lord is God, and he has made his light shine upon us." (Psalm 118:27)

Discussion Questions
1. Have you ever had someone give you a mean look? How did it make you feel? How did you respond to that person? How did it make

you feel when someone smiled at you? Do you smile back? Explain.

2. Think about David's life in the Bible. As you consider the many stories about his life do you recall the occasions when you believe David smiled? Explain.

3. Are you living a life that makes God smile? Every area of your life? If not, what area(s) do you need to work on so that God can smile? Be honest with yourself.

Prayer

Father, I bless your name because you are so good to me. You are better to me then I even realize. And, because you are I should bless your name everyday. You love me even when I don't deserve it. And, so I smile because you shine the light of your face upon me. God, I want you to be Lord over every area of my life. I want to be holy and pleasing to you. Thank you for smiling on me. I pray that I can make you smile all the time and that your smile would cause me to smile even more. In Jesus' name I pray. Amen.

Reflection

_____

_____

_____

_____

_____

LIGHT OF MY LIFE

"Since we belong to the day, let us be self controlled." (1 Thess. 5:8)

Have you ever been in a room when all the lights went out? When you have to stand in the darkness it can be scary, paralyzing, and confusing. You hesitate, at first, not knowing what to do. Then, you search to find a light switch. You move with caution so you don't trip over something. Depending upon how you're wired, you might panic or lose all sense of direction because of the darkness. You might completely lose it and never figure out what to do.

Now, many people may never get stranded in the dark like this, but many walk around with a darkened mind. "They are darkened in their understanding." (Eph. 4:18) This happens when we worry, stress, and get confused by doing things outside of God's will. But, worry, stress, and confusion are not from God. (I Cor. 14:33) God has given us a mind of Christ. (I Cor. 2:16; 2 Tim. 1:17) Moreover, you have the light of life in you. (John 8:12) His word is a lamp to your feet and a light to your path. (Psa. 119:105) God is marvelous!

The next time you feel worried about your job situation or marriage, you can be certain that God will be there with you. When you feel anxious about being able to provide for your family or caring for your children, God will be there. And when you feel confused about a major decision or where you are in your life, stop, get still, and get in touch with God's presence inside of you. The light from His face will shine down upon you so that you will be a light for the whole world to see.

Are you struggling with some area of self control? Lust? Pornography? Are you stressing, worrying, or concerned about something? If that's you, then, perhaps, you need to chat with God. He is your light and your salvation.

Affirmation
God, you are the Light Of My Life, when:
- I am walking alone in the dark
- I am frustrated, afraid, or feeling doubt
- I am confused or uncertain about life
- I am feeling anxious or starting to worry
- I need to make an important decision

Meditation Verse
"The light shines in the darkness." John 1:5

Discussion Questions
1. What area(s) of sin are you struggling with in your life right now? In what area of your mind is your understanding darkened? What can you do (or are you doing) to move into the light?
2. What is causing you to worry, stress, or be anxious? Explain. Locate various Scripture verses in the Bible related to each topic and meditate on those verses.

3. How do you walk in the light everyday? Explain. Can you do better? What do you need that you don't presently have to walk consistently everyday?

Prayer

I come before you Lord to bask in your presence. There's no other place I'd rather be. In your presence I find peace and tranquility. There I also find strength because of your might and power. I rest knowing that you are the One and Only God. I fear nothing or no one because you are my protection and covering. I have no fear, doubt, or worry because none of those things come from you. I pray that I would walk in the light everyday. I pray for your guidance. In Jesus' name. Amen.

Reflection

_____

_____

_____

_____

_____

SPEAK THROUGH ME

"For out of the overflow of the heart the
mouth speaks." (Matt. 12:34)

Have you ever been at a loss for words? You
initially knew what you wanted to say, but almost
in an instant, the words disappeared. Have you ever
stumbled or stammered while speaking? You were
giving a speech or talking to a group and something
caused you forget your words. Have you ever just
failed to convey what you wanted to get across? You
knew what you wanted to say, but the words just
did not come across as you wanted them to. Well, if
you've ever had any of these challenges, then let God
guide every word you speak.

Jesus said that out of the abundance of the heart,
the mouth speaks. (Matt. 12:34) He goes on to say,
"The good man brings good things out of the good
stored up in him, and the evil man brings evil things
out of the evil stored up in him." (Matt. 12:35) Thus,
whatever has been placed in your heart will flow out
of your mouth. So on the one hand, if you are angry,
doubtful, or uncertain, then your words will reflect
that when you speak. Your heart will be filled with
anger and depressed thoughts and your mouth will
overflow with the same. But, on the other hand, if
you have something good to say it's because you
have good things trapped in your heart.

Jesus said it like this: "But I tell you that men will
have to give an account on the day of judgment for

every careless word they have spoken. For by your words you will be acquitted, and by your words you will be condemned." (Matt. 12:36-37) So how do you get to a place of having only good things trapped in your heart? Well, you must read God's word daily. You will need to deposit the truth in your heart. The Truth is filled with purity, love, hope, and goodness. As a result, your heart will overflow with purity, love, hope and goodness. Then, you will no longer have to worry about searching for the right words. God will always provide you with the right words to speak. His Word will flow out of your mouth.

Affirmation

God, Speak Through Me when:
- I am seemingly at a loss for words
- I am feeling as if I have nothing to say
- You desire to speak to others through me
- I need the right words to share with my spouse
- I am feeling angry, bitter, or frustrated

Meditation Verse

"The mouth of the righteous man is a fountain of life." (Proverbs 10:11)

Discussion Questions

1. What do you do to put good things in your heart? What habits or practices do you have to make good words a daily reality? Explain.

2. How can you influence others to speak good words? How does it make you feel when you hear someone yelling, cursing, etc. Explain.

3. Find a few verses in the Bible that speak about the 'mouth.' What does God say about people who speak good things versus those who speak bad or evil things.

Prayer

Lord, I come humbly before you because you are the living God. It's awesome to be able to come into your presence. I come surrendering all to you, but specifically my heart and mouth. I know that I don't always allow the right things to enter my heart and so I can't blame my mouth for what it says. But, I know that with your strength I can over come. I don't desire to have bad things flow from my lips. So I ask that you would soften my heart and make it like yours. I only want to make good deposits so the over-flow will only be good. I surrender my mouth to you and ask that you'd give me the right words to speak. I do it all in Jesus' name. Amen.

Reflection

_____

_____

_____

_____

_____

Your Grace is Sufficient

"My grace is sufficient for you, for my
power is made perfect in weakness.
Therefore, I will boast all the more gladly
about my weaknesses, so that Christ's power
may rest on me." (2 Cor. 12:9)

All of us have moments when we feel weak. Men are not excluded. At times, we feel powerless over our circumstances. But, have you ever considered that it's at that time that you are actually strong? It doesn't seem to make sense. In fact, it's counter intuitive, but it's true. It's in those moments when you feel alone that God is still there working in a powerful way. God sent you and me His Holy Spirit to give us power. (See Acts) It's the same power that raised Christ from the dead. (Eph. 1:19-20)

The Apostle Paul had achieved a lot in his life, but he understood that there was power in weakness. He realized that the God's Spirit had been sent to do a miraculous work for him and others. You must realize that God has sent us power through His Spirit. "Greater is He that is in you, than he that is in the world." (I John 4:4) You must trust God in moments when you feel powerless. He is residing in you. He is with you always as a child of God.

God wants you to know that in moments of weakness he is in control even though it seems like things are out of control. When you have had major surgery know that He is in control. When you have been injured in an auto accident realize that He is in control. When you have to give a speech and you are fearful of public speaking know that He is in control. When you are hired for a job and you have great credentials, but you are the low man on the totem pole know that He is in control. The next time you are feeling weak or powerless, tell yourself, "I serve the living God who lives in me and works through me. Is His grace sufficient for you?

Affirmation

God, Your Grace Is Sufficient:
- When I am experiencing a moment of weakness
- In the midst of my recovery from alcohol addiction
- When I am tired and weary
- In the midst of trying circumstances
- When I want to give up and quit

Meditation Verse

"But by the grace of God I am what I am...yet not I, but the grace of God that was with me." (1 Cor. 10)

Discussion Questions

1. Think about when you experienced your greatest moment of weakness. Did you feel powerless or alone? How did you get through the situation? How did God help you get through? Share your testimony with someone or in a small group.

2. How does God take a weakness and make it a strength?

3. Do you believe that God is living in you? Explain. Is His grace sufficient for you? Are you content to let Him work out things out according to His plan for your life?

Prayer

Father, your grace is sufficient for me. You strengthen my strengths and make my weaknesses into strengths. You know about every detail of my life. You know what's going to happen before it ever does. Therefore, I can trust you in every situation even at when I am at my weakest. I know that all things are possible through you who gives me strength. I believe that you will work out everything according to your plan for me. Bless you. In Jesus' name. Amen.

Reflection

_____

_____

_____

_____

_____

SPEAK TO ME

"Whether you turn to the right or to the
left, your ears will hear a voice behind you,
saying, "This is the way, walk in it."
(Isaiah 30:21)

Have you ever found yourself not knowing what to do? Have you ever hesitated about making a decision? If so, then you are like many men who ask, "What do I do?" You have an important decision to make and you can't afford to be wrong. What should you do? Where should you turn?

No matter your situation or circumstance, you can turn to the Lord and ask Him for direction and guidance. God doesn't see things the same way you do. He knows what you are going to ask. He knows the outcome of the situation before you ask. And, He knows whether there will be good or bad consequences. God sees the bigger picture and directs you down the right road. When you are obedient and listen, He will speak through a rock, a friend, a spouse, through His word, or whatever means He chooses. He will tell you which direction you should or shouldn't go.

If you listen, He will guide you step by step along the way. All you have to do is listen to hear His voice and follow Him. When He speaks to you, He will guide you by His peace. When He speaks, He will guide you by His goodness. When He speaks, He will guide you by His sincerity. When He speaks, He will guide you by His love. Step by step along the way, He will show you what to do. Ask God to speak to you today. He is waiting to give you the guidance that you need.

Affirmation

Lord, Speak To Me:

- About my current situation or circumstances
- To help me overcome lust and sexual addiction
- Because I need your direction and guidance
- To tell me the path I should take in the future
- Because I really need to hear your voice

Meditation Verse

"If anyone hears my voice and opens the door, I will come in and eat with him, and be with me." (Rev. 3:20)

Discussion Questions

1. How does God speak to you in your life? Audible voice? Do you hear from Him regularly, occasionally, rarely, or not at all? Do you know His voice? How does He communicate to you?

2. How did God speak to His people in the Old Testament? New Testament? Does He still speak to you and me today? If so, how and how do you know?

3. Where do you go to hear God's voice? A private place away from the busyness of life?

When you hear from Him what do you do?
Immediately take action or wait? Explain.

Prayer

Lord, I want to hear your voice. I want to speak
to you. I pray that you'd take me to a place where
I can hear you more clearly. I don't hear from you
often because I am either too busy and need to get
still or because I really don't know your voice as well
as I think I do. I pray for your guidance, direction,
peace, and love no matter my circumstances. You
know everything before it happens so I desire to hear
from you. In Jesus' name. Amen.

Reflection

_____

_____

_____

_____

_____

LET ME TO BE STILL

"Be still, and know that I am God."
(Psalm 46:10)

For many of us life can seem very busy. Your home telephone rings with calls from family. Your cellular telephone rings with calls from friends. Your work telephone rings with calls from co-workers. When you get to work, you log onto the computer, check your emails, and attend to whatever you have on your plate for the day. Busy, busy, busy.

You have to give attention to family, work, and a busy social life. You come home to the sound of the washing machine, television, beeping of the micro-wave, hammering of construction, dog barking, and much more. You are surrounded by noise and busy-ness, which at times can seem like chaos.

You have so much to attend to that often you don't make time for God. You tell Him how much you love Him, but you push Him away because you won't slow down and get still. The secret to intimacy is finding a quiet place where it's just you and the Lord. An instant in his presence, can take you from noise to a secret chamber of tranquility where He can help you refocus. A moment with Him can take you from knowing about Him to a truly personal relationship with Him.

Once you arrive in His presence, you then get still and know how much He loves you. You realize that you are protected, cared for, and treasured. The

Lord will provide everything you need. (Phil. 4:19) He will never leave you or forsake you. (Heb. 13:5) Be still and know that He is God. (Ps. 46:10)

Affirmation

God, Let Me Be Still when:
- I get consumed with the busyness of life
- So I can receive insight and direction
- My kids are acting like the devil's children
- I need to find a quiet place of peace
- So that I can know you are the One true God

Meditation Verse

"Be still before the Lord and wait patiently on him." (Psalm 37:7)

Discussion Questions

1. How would you describe your life? Busy? Where do you spend most of your time? What do you spend most of your time doing? How much time do you spend devoted to work, family, and personal things? To the things of God?

2. Where do you spend time alone with God? A retreat? Private room? Church sanctuary? How do you spend your time alone with God? What do you do? Is it productive time? If so, how and why?

3. If you aren't spending enough time with God how can you make a change to do so?

Prayer

Jehovah God, I rejoice when I am in your presence. I glory when I have time alone with you. In your presence, there is peace, power and tranquility. When I am alone with you I truly know that there is none like you. When I am alone with you I recognize that you are God alone and there is no other god before you. Thank you in advance for letting me slow down so I can enter your presence. I love you. In Jesus' name. Amen.

Reflection

_____

_____

_____

_____

_____

YOU ARE MY ROCK

"The Lord is my rock, my fortress and my
deliverer; my God is my rock, in whom I
take refuge." (Psalm 18:2)

Have you ever felt helpless or hopeless? Have
you encountered moments when it seemed like life
was just tossing you backward and forward? Your
emotions overwhelmed, threatening to drag you
deep in despair? Or, perhaps, it seemed like life was
moving so quickly you couldn't keep up? One day
running into the next. Days, months, years going by
faster and faster. You never seem to have enough
time in a day to get anything done. In fact, you feel
like you're losing time everyday! Does any of this
sound familiar?

Well, if so, know that God wants to be your rock.
(Ps. 18:2) He wants to help you stay rooted in all
situations. You've heard the phrase, "hard as a rock?"
That's how God wants you to see your life. He wants
to be the solid foundation that supports everything
you do. (Ps. 18:46) He wants to be your super glue
that holds everything together. God wants you to
know that He remains unshakeable in every situation. He stands firm and solid. (Ps. 62:2)

Do you know anyone who can give you a firm
foundation? No, definitely not! But, God is that
someone who can and does provide a solid foundation. He can provide support if you just need to rest,
if you want to slow down, or take a break. He can

be the rock of refuge or fortress you can run to. (Ps. 31:2) You can hide under the shadow of His wing and there you can find peace, protection, or comfort. (Ps. 91) God wants to be the rock of your salvation. (Ps. 62:2)

Affirmation

God, You Are My Rock:
- In times of trouble
- When I am feeling scared and alone
- In moments of temptation
- When I need someone to hold onto
- In stressful situations

Meditation Verse

"The Lord is my rock, my fortress and my deliverer; my God is my rock, in whom I take refuge." (2 Sam. 22:2)

Discussion Questions

1. Have you ever encountered a time when you desperately needed the Lord? If so, what did you do? Pray? Read the Bible? Share with others in the church? Should we only call on Him when we have an urgent need? Why or why not?

2. What does it mean to "take refuge" in the Lord? How do you do it?

3. What are you going through right now? Stress? Loneliness? Anxiety? Other emotional struggle? Read Ps. 18:2, reflect, and meditate on the verse.

Prayer

Lord, I run to you in good times and bad. When I am feeling scared or lonely you are there. When I am suffering in pain you are there. When I am feeling tempted you are there. When I simply need someone to hold onto you are there. When I am feeling the stress of daily living you are there. You are my rock. You are my refuge. You are my fortress. You are my strong tower. Lord, you are the rock of my salvation. Thank you for watching over me. In Jesus' name. Amen.

Reflection

_____

_____

_____

_____

_____

KEEP ME SAFE

"If you make the Most High your dwelling
- even the Lord, who is my refuge – then no
harm will befall you, no disaster will come
near your tent." (Psalm 91:9-10)

Have you ever been scared? Your car broke down on a dark road out in nowheresville. You flew on a plane for the very first time. You climbed to the highest point of a ledge overlooking the ocean and one misstep could cause you to fall. You observed a person prowling around homes in your neighborhood. You must depart for a trip and leave your family behind. Perhaps, you've been hurt in a relationship and you have fear of being hurt again.

Fortunately, there is a place you can turn that can remove all fear and doubt. God is there for you. He wants to be your protection. He wants you to be your refuge and fortress. (Ps. 91:2) He wants to be your ultimate hiding place. (Ps. 32:7) God can keep you safe from any harm. He will provide a hedge of protection and give His angels watch over you. When life presents times of fear – which man will experience – the Lord is there for you so that no disaster will come near your tent. (Psalm 91:9-10)

What are you scared of? Is there something causing you fear? Are you faced with potential job loss? Is your spouse threatening to divorce you? Did you recently lose a loved one? Turn to God and ask Him to help to keep you from falling.

Affirmation

Lord, Keep Me Safe:
- When the enemy tries to over take me
- When man tries to cause my feet to stumble
- When fear and doubt confront me
- When danger is all around me
- Because you are my refuge and fortress

Meditation Verse

"The name of the Lord is a strong tower; the righteous run to it and are safe." (Prov. 18:10)

Discussion Questions

1. Think about a time when you were scared. How did you react to the situation? Good? Bad? Is fear still gripping you today? Have you been able to leave the past behind you? If so, how did you give the situation over to the Lord? Explain.

2. In what area(s) does fear drive your life? Explain.

3. Has the Lord ever kept you safe in a dangerous situation? If so, how? Explain.

Prayer

Lord Jesus, I find total safety in you. You keep me from the fowler's snare. You protect me from the arrows that fly by day and night. You don't let my feet stumble. Although many around me may fall you allow me to remain standing. I pray that fear and doubt would not overtake me. Even when there's danger all around, I pray that you'd keep me safe. Blessing and honor to your name. Amen.

Reflection

_____

_____

_____

_____

_____

You Are My Hope

"Why so downcast, O my soul? Why so
disturbed within me? Put your hope in
God, for I will yet praise him, my Savior."
(Psalm 42:5)

Have you ever had a time when you lost hope?
You felt depressed? You know when someone hits
rock bottom because you can see it on their face.
In fact, many people are experiencing these kinds
of emotions today. Feeling downtrodden because
someone has died? Depressed and tired of the daily
rigors of the workplace? Facing a broken or failed
relationship? Perhaps, experiencing difficulty in
dealing with a family member or friend?

If you've been facing a situation that has been
going on for far too long. If you've grown tired and
weary. If you can't see any real resolution. If you've
concluded that all hope is gone. If that's you, then
you need to know that there's still good news! What
is it? There's always hope in God. He has a plan for
your life. His plan includes hope in your future. (Jer.
29:11)

Even when circumstances seem to indicate
otherwise, God is still there! Thus, you can set hope
against despair because God is a miracle worker. He
can bring you out of hopelessness. He can bring you
out of situations that seem hopeless to all men. God
is our hope. He is there no matter how things might
appear.

Why be without hope? Hope is just a prayer away. Put your trust in God today and He will answer you.

Affirmation

Lord, You Are My Hope:
- In the midst of my addictive behavior
- While my marriage seems to be failing
- When I am feeling hopeless and in despair
- Because you have a plan for my life
- When I am at the end of myself

Meditation Verse

"We have this hope as an anchor for the soul, firm and secure." (Hebrews 6:19)

Discussion Questions

1. Have you ever lost hope? Discuss the circumstances with someone or in a small group? How are you feeling today? Explain.
2. Think about God's plan for your life? How has He encouraged you along your Christian journey? How has God given you hope?
3. Does hope have a purpose? Why does God give us hope and a future. (See Jer. 29:11) How do you interpret the verse? Explain.

Prayer

Father in heaven, I come before you to bless your name. I honor, worship, and adore you. When I am feeling hopeless I turn to you. For in you there's great hope. There's hope for times of despair. Hope for hopeless situations. There's hope when I don't know which way to turn. Hope for today. Hope for tomorrow. Hope for the future. Thank you in advance for causing my mind to shift from my own selfish thoughts to Christ-centered ones that glorify you. Help me breakthrough wherever I am stuck right now. In Jesus' name. Amen.

Reflection

_____

_____

_____

_____

_____

I BECAME A MAN

"When I became a man, I put childish ways
behind me." (I Cor. 13:11b)

Do you remember the guy from high school that
dated all the pretty girls? He was known as a "player."
He played the field and had his pick of the ladies. He
thought he was "the man"? How about the guy who
was hanging out drinking and smoking? He thought
he was in with the "cool" crowd? How about the jock
that excelled athletically, but never went to class? He
did not learn much in school, but he graduated with
you, right? You probably remember someone in one
of those categories. But, a lot of things people did in
their youth was childish.

Unfortunately, as you grow older you can still
do some of those childish things – even though you
are supposed to be a grown adult. For example, you
continue to play the field – even though you know
you are living outside of God's will. You continue to
smoke, drink, do drugs, and hang out with the wrong
crowd because you are trying to fit in. You continue
to fail to apply yourself fully at work, school, etc.
– never really measuring up to your full potential.

The reality is that real men aren't defined by how
many women they can date, whether they drink or
smoke, or what their social status is. Real men are
defined by how they follow God in every area of
their life. Leaving the childish things in the past and
striving for the adult things ahead, you strive to attain

to the higher calling God has for you heavenward. As you move from spiritual childhood to adolescence (keeping adulthood in view), you realize that God has new things for you to see and do. His desire is that you'd leave the things of the past behind and move into the newness of what he has for you. Put off your old self because you are a new creation in Christ Jesus. (Col. 3:8-10)

Affirmation

Father, I Became A Man:
- So that I could be pleasing to you
- So that I would no longer be a child
- So that I will walk in a new way
- So that I can leave the old things behind
- So I can be more like your son Jesus Christ

Meditation Verse

"Oh Lord Almighty, blessed is the man who trusts you." Psalm 84:12

Discussion Questions

1. What does it mean to be a man? Has the definition of manhood changed since 1920? 1940? 1960? 1980? How do you define manhood?

2. Are there some childish things that you are doing now? Not speaking to someone? Acting irresponsibly? Is it time to make a change? Explain?

3. Share a testimonial about how you've moved from childlike ways to thinking and acting

like a man? How have you changed? How did the change happen? Explain.

Prayer

Father God help me to grow and mature into the likeness of your son Jesus Christ. You have not called me to drink milk like a child. Rather, you desire that I put away childish things and grow into the Christian adult you've call me to be. I pray that I'd grow in increasing measure so I can be more like you. Teach what it means to be a child of God. In Jesus name. Amen.

Reflection

_____

_____

_____

_____

_____

GENTLE AS A LAMB

"Your gentleness has made me great."
(Psalm 18:35)

People in our world have often equated gentleness with weakness. Sometimes, it's true. But very often, it is simply not the case and couldn't be any further from the truth. In fact, if you've lived on the planet long enough, you understand that this principle runs head first into our earthy way of doing things. Many people think they have to be first in line, have an overpowering personality, or be machismo to get a point across or accomplish some goal. Status and rank is important to a lot of people. But, the Bible says that those who are first on earth will be last in heaven, and the last first. (Mark 10:31; 2 Cor. 12:9) Do you get the picture?

Gentleness is an attribute on which Christ placed a great value. This trait can often appear as a quiet confidence. Gentle people know they don't have to overpower someone to reach or motivate them. They realize that they can encourage others with kind words and a gentle spirit. They realize that a gentle answer turns away wrath. (Psa. 15:1) They understand that they ought to be completely humble and gentle, (Eph. 4:2), in every area of life. Gentleness flies in the face of how ordinary society does things. But, then, Christians are not called to be ordinary. God's desire is that we would live Spirit-filled lives that would cause us to be extraordinary.

Gentleness is an attribute that you cannot afford to be without unless you want God not to be gentle to you. (1 Cor. 4:21) Rather than experience God's wrath because of your sin, you can receive God's love through His wonderful grace – a free gift for everyone who extends themselves to Him. God reached down to us to save us from our sins – past, present, and future. Then, He gave His fruit of gentleness so we could grow and mature. We ought to take hold of that fruit and let it ripen in our life. Then, our gentleness truly becomes God's gentleness.

Affirmation

Lord, Gentle As A Lamb:
- To my wife and children
- When I speak to my co-workers
- Although my upbringing has been tough
- So I don't experience your wrath
- Because greater is He who is in me

Meditation Verse

"Be completely humble and gentle." (Ephesians 4:2)

Discussion Questions

1. How can you explain the tension between gentleness and how most of us live our everyday life?
2. Have you ever been perceived as being too gentle? To passive? To kind? Has your gentleness ever been viewed as weakness? Explain.

3. How can you work to make your gentleness grow? What area(s) of your life need the most work? Be honest with yourself.

Prayer

Father, you make me complete with your love. Thank you for always showing me your ever-wonderful mercy and grace. I desire to be more like you. I pray that the fruit of the Spirit would be manifested in my life through the power of the Holy Spirit. One particular fruit is gentleness, for which there is no replacement. Let me saturate myself with gentleness so I might know what it means to walk in your ways. I pray that you would fill me fresh and anew. In Jesus' name. Amen.

Reflection

_____

_____

_____

_____

_____

HELP ME

"In my distress I screamed to the Lord for
his help. And he heard me from heaven; my
cry reached his ears." (Psalm 18:6)

Are you in a challenging situation right now? Has
fear gripped you in a way like never before? Do you
need to turn to someone for assistance? Well, you
may never encounter a situation where your life is
hanging on the edge. But, chances are that many men
will find themselves in extremely difficult circumstances at some point in life. During those moments,
you will need immediate help because you will find
yourself in a situation you won't be able to get out of
by yourself.

Aren't you glad to know that God hears your cry.
(Ex. 2:23) He's available to you by simply calling
His name. Unlike a relative or friend, He is with you
all the time. He will never leave you or forsake you.
(Heb. 13:5) He hears your despairing cry in your
distress. (Isa. 30:19) And, he not only hears you, but
promises you will find help in response to your call.
He turns His ears toward you and He listens. God
hears you from heaven and your cries reach His ears.
And, He responds to provide for your need. (Ibid)
He will provide wisdom, insight, or understanding
in how to resolve your difficulty. He will give you
exactly what you need, at exactly the right time. God
is your help.

Affirmation

Lord, Help Me:
- In my most challenging moments in life
- When I am feeling low and depressed
- Through the problems in my marriage
- When I am facing serious health issues
- Because you are my help in times of trouble

Meditation Verse

"But I have had God's help to this very day, and so I stand here and testify to small and great alike." (Acts 26:22)

Discussion Questions

1. Describe a challenging situation that you've encountered in the recent past or that you are going through right now? Who can you call for assistance?

2. What has been the most challenging moment in your life? How did you overcome the situation? Did you rely on others? Turn to God? Read and mediate on Psalm 18:6 and share your thoughts with someone or in a small group.

3. What do you believe are the three most challenging situations a person can face in life? Are some of the examples you shared similar or different from stories in the Bible? Explain.

Prayer

Lord, I call on your name in both good and bad times. I pray that you'd hear my cry in times of great need. Hear me when I am feeling lowly and depressed. Hear me when I am have difficulty being a good husband or dad. Hear me when I am hurting. Hear me when I am experiencing extreme health issues. I call on your name because I know that there is no other name that brings healing and restoration. I pray this prayer in Jesus' name. Amen.

Reflection

_____

_____

_____

_____

_____

LET GO OF THE PAST

"As far as the east is from the west,
so far has he removed our transgressions
from us." (Psalm 103:12)

Did you know that you are not your past? You are not your feelings, hurts, or pains. Those emotions are not supposed to define who you are as a person. You've failed, made huge mistakes, been neglected, abused, or mistreated, but that's not who you are. You are God's child and He doesn't see you that way. He sees you as His son or daughter whom He loves. He sees you through the eyes of a loving Father.

Knowing this, you must take those things that seem to be keeping you stuck and give them over to Him. Only the Master can heal the hurt and pain of your past. You allow him to enter into your life when you forgive those who have hurt you and caused you pain. He also enters when you learn to forgive yourself. You must be a partaker in the abundance of His forgiveness. When you partake, He allows you to bask in his wonderful presence and get more deeply rooted in your true identity – being like Jesus Christ. You must let Him remove the dark spots in your heart so you can become a whole person.

Now, God's Word doesn't say that you have to forget the past. But, He surely doesn't want you to wallow in a place of self-pity and remain stuck in a bad place forever. That would be counter-productive to His purpose and plan for your life. God wants you to get up, brush yourself off, and get back into the game. Although at times, you may feel hurt and pain, the Lord can remove it in the blink of an eye. He wants you to be ready to receive the blessings He has for you. Let go of the past.

Affirmation

God, help me Let God Of The Past:
- So I can understand who you are
- Because you don't want me to stay stuck
- And free me from torment
- When I am reminded of it
- So I can be whole

Meditation Verse

"Forget the former things; do not dwell on the past. See, I am doing a new thing!" (Isa. 43:18-19)

Discussion Questions

1. In what area(s) of your life are you stuck? You just can't get beyond a past hurt? Have you shared with someone or in a small group? With God?

2. How do you see yourself right now? Are you healthy emotionally? Spiritually?

3. How has the Lord guided you through the difficult challenges of the past? Do you have a testimony about God's mercy and grace? What advice would you give someone who is stuck in their past?

Prayer

Father, your love endures forever. I hang onto the hope of my future, which is you Lord. I surrender everything that I have yet to surrender. I give you all of my heart, emotions, and feelings. I cast all of my cares and concerns on you. Take my insecurities, deficiencies, and idiosyncrasies. I want to be like you Lord. Transform me into the likeness of your son Jesus Christ. I am a new creation and I want to walk in my newness. I let go of my past and ask you to hold my hand as I move forward.

Reflection

_____

_____

_____

_____

_____

Bring Me Comfort

"As a mother comforts her child, so will I comfort you; and you will be comforted."
(Isaiah 66:13)

Have you ever felt pain in your life? Most of us have at one time or another. Remember when you were a young lad. You had an accident on your bicycle, skateboard, etc. You had some minor scrapes and bruises, but there was also some pain. As adults, we encounter pain too. It may be chronic, or perhaps, a periodic ache? Maybe it's a result of divorce, abandonment, job loss, or other loss or failure. We don't typically understand pain as a good thing or God thing, but often it can be.

Think about when you are working out trying to get into shape. Your body can experience pain. Perhaps, you're running to try to push your body beyond its limit. You may experience pain associated with your workout. But, the pain you feel is not a sign that something is wrong. Even though your body tells you to slow down or stop, it's often a sign that you've exhausted the muscle you are trying to build up. The pain associated with muscle fatigue is part of the process of building muscle. You can experience emotional pain too as a result of any number of life situations. The important thing is having an appropriate response to whatever it is you are going through.

Thankfully, we can respond to pain by running to the God of all Comfort before we do more damage to our health. Jesus promised that He would never leave us or forsake us. (Heb. 13:5) He is a Comforter who can ease the pains of life. (Isa. 66:13) There's no pain that He cannot ease. Although, at times we walk through what seems to be the Valley of the Shadow of Death, our God brings comfort as we walk and until we reach the other side. (Ps. 23)

Affirmation

Oh God, Bring Me Comfort:
- Through the pain of a broken relationship
- So I don't quit running the race
- When I experience emotional or physical pain
- So that I might be able to comfort someone else
- Because you are a healer and comforter

Meditation Verse

"O my Comforter in sorrow, my heart is faint within me. [Listen to my cry]." (Jer. 8:18)

Discussion Questions

1. What does it mean to provide comfort to someone? Do you recall a scenario when you comforted someone? Someone comforted you? Explain.
2. What's involved in God's role as Comforter? Why does He bring us comfort? Is comfort

about making you feel good or something else?

3. Have you experienced pain in your life? What was the root cause of the pain? What was the impact of the pain? Positive? Negative? What did you learn from your experience? Was there good in the pain? If so, explain.

Prayer

God, I know that you are a great and mighty God. I know that you are with me despite the pain I experience in my life. I believe that you use everything as a tool for your glory. I pray that you would bring comfort during the most challenging times of my life. You heal broken relationships, you erase physical pain, you alleviate emotional imbalance, and you restore spiritual emptiness. You are the one true Comforter. I love you. In Jesus' name. Amen.

Reflection

_____

_____

_____

_____

_____

I RUN TO YOU

"You are my hiding; you will protect me
from trouble and surround me with songs of
deliverance." (Psalm 32:7)

Men run and hide in so many things. You can
pour yourself into your work to try to avoid things
you don't want to deal with. You can hide in alcohol
and drugs trying to escape from reality. You can hide
in sex (outside of God's will) trying to make you feel
good about yourself even when you really don't. Too
many men run to too many of the wrong things trying
to find safety, protection, and answers.

Men can be like little kids playing hide-and-go-
seek. You think you'll never be discovered. But, the
Bible says, the enemy is like a roaring lion seeking
whom he will devour. (I Peter 5:8) The devil has his
eye on you. He's had you on the run and as result
you've been pouring yourself into all the wrong
things. These things have been empty and have led
to more hurt, pain, loneliness, sorrow, depression,
and more.

My friend, the Father is watching you. He wants
you to know that He is the perfect hiding place. If you
need protection you can find it under the shadow of
His wing. (Ps. 91) He will not let anyone or anything
harm you. (Ibid) He keeps you safe from the fowler's
snare (Ps. 91) and anything that might threaten your
existence. God has you covered in the day and night.

(Ibid) He keeps your enemies from causing you harm (Psa. 91; Psa. 23:5).

What has you on the run? Are you living outside of God's will? Where do you look to find your safety and protection? Worldly things or God? If you are feeling empty, hurt, or lonely, perhaps, you should give God a try. Run to God! He is your hiding place.

Affirmation

Lord, I Run to You:
- When it seems like all hell is breaking loose
- When everything seems to be going wrong
- When it seems my back is up against the wall
- When my enemies are vigorously pursuing me
- When the odds are stacked up against me in life

Meditation Verse

"Therefore, since we are surrounded by such a great cloud of witnesses...let us run with perseverance the race marked out for us." (Heb. 12:1)

Discussion Questions

1. What do you do (or have you done) to escape from reality? Be honest. Did it glorify God? Was it consistent with God's will for your life? Why or why not?

2. How do you respond when your back is up against a wall? Do you try to fix things? Do you consult with God? Be honest. If you don't

typically consult with God first, how can you become more consistent doing so?

3. Do you spend more time running from God or to God? Examine yourself and share your response with someone or in a small group.

Prayer

Lord, I run to you when it seems like nothing is going right. I run to you in the day and night. I run to you when my back is up against the wall. I run to you when I've taken a fall. I run to you when I am being pursued by my enemies. I run to you when no one wants to be a friend to me. I run to you. In Jesus' name I pray. Amen.

Reflection

_____

_____

_____

_____

_____

SPEAK THROUGH ME LORD

"The Holy Spirit will give you the right
words even as you are standing there."
(Luke 12:12)

Lord, I don't know what to say? I am completely at a loss? Have you ever struggled to find the right words to share? Perhaps, it was someone who you were visiting who was sick and they asked, "So if there is a God why am I here in the hospital suffering?" Or maybe it was an encounter with someone who asked about your faith and you had to evangelize to them. You just couldn't find the right words. Or maybe you had to share at a meeting or with a group, but you weren't sure whether your words would be appropriate to share?

Well, there's good news. You don't have to do it alone. The Holy Spirit will give you the right words even as you are standing there. God will use you to bless others with your words if you follow His leading and prompting. The blessings often flow out of our mouth and touch the ears of those meant to hear. When we ask God to use us, He tends to do so in a powerful way. We think at times that what we have to share isn't going to be good or insightful for others. But when God gets a hold of it, He uses it to bless other people in way we can not conceive.

God doesn't want us to be empty on words. He wants us to fill up on His word so we will be ready to speak. When we are in the Word, He will give us a rich deposit that will overflow in our heart. When we speak . . . out flows the joyous seed planted allowing Him to speak through us because we followed His lead. Ask God to give you the right words to speak and the stream from your mouth will be river of life from the one, true, living God.

Affirmation

Speak Through Me Lord:
- So I can speak the right words
- So I can be a blessing to others
- Because your Word brings life
- So I can be a vessel used by you
- So I can imitate Jesus Christ

Meditation Verse

"But the Counselor, the Holy Spirit, whom the Father will send in my name, will teach you all things and will remind you of everything." (John 14:26)

Discussion Questions

1. Have you ever had a moment when you were at a loss for words? What did you do? How did you react? Embarrassed? How would you handle things if you had a chance to do it over again?

2. Think about a time when you believe God spoke through you to someone else or a group? Describe the circumstances. What was the impact on others? How does God speak through you?

3. How is it possible for God to speak through a human being? Does He speak through each person the same way? Has God ever spoken to you through someone else? Preacher? Friend? Relative? Non-believer? Explain. How did the words impact you?

Prayer

Father, I pray for the right words to speak in every situation. I realize that I don't have to do it on my own. I can always consult with you. I want to be a blessing to others and I desire to be a vessel used by you because I want to be like your son, Jesus Christ. I pray that you would guide my tongue and direct the words of my mouth. Let the words of my mouth bless your name at all times. In Jesus' name. Amen.

Reflection

_____

_____

_____

_____

_____

GIVE ME YOUR PEACE

"My peace I now give and bequeath to
you. Not as the world gives . . . . Do not let
your hearts be troubled, neither let them be
afraid." (John 14:27)

Many people worry about their job, the next
paycheck, and how they will feed their family. Men
worry because they are often the primary provider
and relish the role. But, can you blame men for
worrying in today's unsettled society? With mass
layoffs, firings, and companies going out of business,
it's no wonder why we bite our nails hoping to hang
onto everything we have. Men must stop allowing
worry to creep up into their lives causing agitation
and frustration.

The fact of the matter is that you don't have to
let worry overtake you. You don't have to become
agitated, frustrated, or unsettled. You certainly cannot
overcome your feelings with your own strength. You
need someone much greater than yourself in whom
you can cast all of your cares and concerns. You need
someone in whom you can put all your trust. That
person would be Jesus Christ.

Jesus has left you with peace. He has left you His
peace. His peace is the kind that you cannot comprehend. His peace is the kind that displaces anxiety and
replaces it with a settled hope. His peace is the kind
that puts a troubled heart at ease. His peace is the
kind that surpasses all human understanding.

When a man becomes settled and knows that God can deliver him from any circumstances, His fears run out and peace runs in. Suddenly, worry loses its power and peace becomes a strong tower. No matter what you're going through. God always causes you to triumph in Christ! (See 2 Cor. 2:14) Find a place of peace today!

Affirmation

Lord, Give Me Your Peace when:

- Circumstances arise that seem insurmountable
- My life seems to be filled with stressful situations
- I am experiencing intense spiritual warfare
- Others around me encounter problems and difficulties
- I feel anger, bitterness, or resentment against someone

Meditation Verse

"Peace I leave with you; my peace I give you. I do not give to you as the world gives. Do not let your hearts be troubled and do not be afraid." (John 14: 27)

Discussion Questions

1. What is causing you to worry? Finances? Job loss? Family issue? Other? How are you dealing with your emotions? Have you talked to anyone about how you are feeling? What's the solution?

2. Think about some aspects of nature that are peaceful. Explain what makes each aspect peaceful? Compare your circumstances to the aspects of nature you've considered. How can you find true peace in your life?

3. Have you ever found a place of peace when you were experiencing turmoil? What did it look like? How did you feel afterward? How did it change you?

Prayer

Father, I enter your presence asking for your peace that surpasses all understanding. When I experience turmoil in my life, I desire your peace. When I have lost a loved one, job, relationship, or have experienced some other loss, I desire your peace. When I am not in my right state of mind because of anger, depression, hostility, or other unhealthy emotion, I desire your peace. Lord, I desire the peace that only you can give. Bless my heart with your love and peace. In Jesus' name. Amen.

Reflection

_____

_____

_____

_____

_____

ADJUST MY ATTITUDE

"You must have the same attitude as that of
Christ Jesus." (Philippians 2:5)

Have you ever heard the saying, "Your attitude
determines your altitude"? Often times, you discover
that's true. If you have a bad attitude, you don't get the
best results. But, if you have a good attitude you often
get positive results. For instance, think about school.
If you didn't believe you could get good grades, pass
a test, or otherwise be successful, then chances are
you experienced a similar outcome. However, if you
always believed and hoped for the best, then chances
are you achieved a similar measure of success.

As it is in the natural so it is in the supernatural.
How high you climb in the things of God is directly
connected to your attitude toward Him. The Bible
tells us that we are to be imitators of Jesus Christ.
(Phil. 2) We are to be good imitators in our words,
deeds, behaviors, actions, and everyday conduct.
We ought to also mimic his attitude – being humble
and adopting the right attitude in all circumstances.
We ought to see the world and our life in the best
possible light, knowing that we are made in God's
image. While considering equality with Him not
something to be grasped, we can recognize that when
we assume the right attitude at school, work, home,
and in everything we do He exalts us to the highest
place. In other words, we achieve ultimate success.

The Bible tells us that we should be careful to obey His every word for "it is God who works in you to will and to act according to His good purpose." (Phil. 2:13) Ask yourself some questions. Do you have a good attitude? Is your heart right? Have you been telling yourself the truth about where you really are? If you aren't sure, let God's Word guide your mind and heart so that you might "continue to work out your salvation with fear and trembling." (Phil. 2:12)

Affirmation
Lord, Adjust My Attitude:
- In moments when I am arrogant and conceited
- While I am in a heated discussion with my spouse
- When I have to wait for something longer than I want
- While I am dealing with co-workers on my job
- So I can grow deeper in my relationship with you

Meditation Verse
"[B]e made new in the attitude of your minds; and put on the new self, created to be like God in true righteousness and holiness." (Eph. 4:23)

Discussion Questions
1. Have you ever had a bad attitude? How did it make you feel? Others? Explain the circum-

stances and think about how you could've responded differently.

2. Have you ever encountered someone with a bad attitude? How did it make you feel? What does the Bible say about bad attitude(s)?

3. How does God want you to adjust your attitude(s)? How can a person make necessary adjustments? Locate several Bible passages that support your position.

Prayer

Almighty God, I give you honor and glory because you are marvelous. Your name is worthy to be exalted. I extol you at all times. You provide me with everything I need in my life. You help me with my physical, mental, spiritual, and emotional needs. You give me the right attitude in heated moments, when I am tired, when I am dealing with stress and anxiety, and when I encounter turmoil in my life. You help me adjust my attitude so I can grow closer to you. It is because of this that I bless you and praise you. I love you, Father. Amen.

Reflection

_____

_____

_____

_____

_____

REACHING THE GOAL

"I press on toward the goal to win the prize."
(Philippians 3:14)

One of the greatest moments in sports history occurred when Michael Phelps won eight Olympic gold medals in different swimming events. He passed a record of seven medals set by Mark Spitz who was known as the greatest swimmer until that time. Michael accomplished his goal with great focus and determination. Can you image how much pressure he must've felt before the first race? It must've been unbearable. Nevertheless, he maintained the right perspective. He did not let anything distract him from reaching his ultimate goal. He wanted to win each race.

The Apostle Paul tells us in Philippians that we must adopt the same perspective in our life. We must take a humble approach to life ("not that I have already obtained this" – v.12), we must keep a singular focus on that which is most important ("But, one thing I do" – v. 13), and run a steady race to obtain our objective ("straining toward what is ahead, I press on toward the goal to win the prize for which God has called me heavenward in Christ Jesus." – vv. 13-14). God wants us to keep our eyes focused on what's really important to Him.

So, if you're feeling the pressure of life or you're distracted by something around you, consider Paul's words. The best way for you to attain to the higher calling set before you is to live a humble life, make certain that Jesus Christ is your foundation, and take daily steps to grow closer to Him. When you allow the distractions of the world to creep in or allow good habits to falter, you can fall short of success. But, when you "live up to what [you] have already attained," (v. 16), you put yourself in the best position to reach your goal.

Affirmation

Lord, I am Reaching the Goal when:
- I give my life over to you completely
- I consider others before myself
- I imitate my Lord and Savior Jesus Christ
- I speak with you everyday
- I walk in the Spirit moment by moment

Meditation Verse

"Are you so foolish? After beginning with the Spirit, are you now trying to attain your goal by human effort?" (Gal. 3:3)

Discussion Questions

1. What is the greatest sports achievement you ever witnessed? How did that person or team accomplish the goal? What did it take to accomplish the goal? What was the ultimate outcome?

2. Are you easily distracted? If so, why? How can you gain better focus?

3. What are your current goals? Are you on track to reach them? What is your plan for success? How will you do it? Explain.

Prayer

Heavenly Father, I fix my eyes on you. I put no one and nothing else before you. You are the desire of my heart. I look not to the left or the right. Rather, I keep my eyes looking forward on the greatest love of my life...you. I desire to have an intimate relationship with you...speaking to you everyday...living for you in every way. You are my all-in-all and I want to walk in the Spirit moment by moment. Teach me your ways all of my days and I will bless your name. In Jesus' name. Amen.

Reflection

_____

_____

_____

_____

_____

GET OUT OF THE WAY

"If anyone would come after me, he must
deny himself and take up his cross and
follow me." (Mark 8:34b)

Do you remember when Michael Jordan played
with the Chicago Bulls? Michael and his teammates
won numerous NBA championships. The players
who played with him were all great and talented
players in their own rite. Several players were some
of the most talented players in the league during that
time. Many of Michael's teammates could've been
starters or significant contributors on other teams.
Playing alongside arguably the greatest player of all
time, however; each player had to set aside his own
personal aspirations (i.e., scoring a lot of points, etc.)
and serve as a support for Michael and role player
for the team.

What an amazing picture that was to see. A group
of highly talented people putting aside personal selfishness to accomplish a common goal. That's the
kind of attitude Jesus told us to adopt. As believers,
we are to deny or disown our self, and put our selfish
needs on the cross. To effectively serve Jesus we
need to get our self out of the way. Getting your self
out of the way is a daily decision, and at times, not an
easy one when our own selfish desires continually try
to get into the picture. The Apostle Paul understood
how to do it. If you read Paul's letters, you see Paul
getting self out of the way. "I affirm, by the boasting

in you which I have in Christ Jesus our Lord, I die daily." (I Cor. 15:31)

In moments when you want to give someone a piece of your mind or when an announcement is made for someone else and you feel yourself knotting up inside, or when your mind is on your to-do-list rather than alert to the person talking to you, you need to deny yourself. Your selfish attitude is so natural that sometimes you won't even notice your impatient behavior. Thus, you need to be conscious of how you are thinking. You also need to be aware of your motives and attitudes before you can get out of your own way. As the saying goes, "You need to check yourself before you wreck yourself." Get out of the way!

Affirmation

Lord, I Get Out of the Way:
- When I consider other's needs before my own
- When I admit that I am denial about my drug abuse
- When I am trying to drive decisions in my life
- When I am having sex but not yet married
- When I confess you are Lord over my entire life

Meditation Verse

"For God did not give you a spirit of timidity, but a spirit of power, of love and of self-discipline." (2 Tim. 1:7)

Discussion Questions

1. In what area(s) of your life are you currently living outside of God's will? What will you do to get on track? Explain.

2. What does the Bible say about self denial? Look up a few verses to help you answer this question. How do you interpret those verses? What does it mean for your life? Why does God tell you to deny yourself?

3. Are there areas of selfishness in your life that you need to work on? What are those areas? Share with an individual or in a small group.

Prayer

Father, first let me ask for forgiveness for all the times I have been selfish. Forgive me for all those moments I have been in your way. Help me to deny myself and take up my cross daily. I pray that I would no longer deny you, but rather surrender my life to you completely. I pray that you would convict me about my wrong attitudes, behaviors, and conduct. I pray that you would make your ways known to me that I would live in accordance with your purpose and plan for my life. Help me get out of your way so that I might be in the center of your will. In Jesus' name. Amen.

Reflection

_____

_____

_____

_____

_____

THINK POSITIVE

"For as he thinketh in his heart, so is he"
(Proverbs 23:7)

Everything you do and say starts in your mind with what you think and believe. To stay sane in a crazy world, it's important to remember that our mind has a great impact on our daily life. The mind is not simple, but rather quite complex. It functions a lot like a computer. The mind can process, store, and share information. And, like a computer, what you put out is a direct result of what you put in.

In many cases, the things we say begin with what we think. We can choose good or bad things to accept. Choosing one or the other will become a way of thinking. If you choose bad thoughts on the one hand, it bears the fruit of poor choices and decisions. If you choose good thoughts on the other hand, it will bear the fruit of positive choices and enriching ideas over negativity.

You must always remember to talk to yourself and tell yourself the truth. Positive self-talk can help you stay positive. It can also help you stay sane. But, what really counts are the words that you speak to yourself. The Truth of God's Word never fails to be the right source of good encouragement. Regardless of what you might be going through, you should always maintain a positive focus. As the Apostle Paul wrote when he was struggling, "my purpose is that they may be encouraged in heart. . . ." (Titus 2:2)

The Apostle Paul knew that his altitude was determined by his attitude. If he wanted to do good things for Christ, he had to have the right things in his heart. To be a blessing to others, he had to encourage himself at times. As a Christian, you put only good things in you when you focus on God. "Whatever you do, whether in word or deed, do it all in the name of the Lord Jesus, giving thanks to God our Father through him." (Col. 3:17)

Affirmation

Lord, I Think Positive when:
- Everything seems to be going wrong
- I am feeling like a worthless failure
- It seems like everyone has forgotten about me
- I am continually arguing with my spouse
- It seems like I am going nowhere on my job

Meditation Verse

"My son, keep your father's commands...[b]ind them upon your heart forever; fasten them around your neck." (Prov. 6:20)

Discussion Questions

1. Think about several reasons why positive thinking is important. Explain. How does the Bible help you think positive? Share a few verses or passages that are an encouragement to you.
2. What Scripture verses can you memorize that will help you with positive self talk when

you need encouragement? Do you tell yourself good things? Do you encourage yourself
regularly? Explain.

3. We receive a lot of negative messages in our
   society today. How do you keep yourself
   from thinking negative thoughts?

Prayer

Lord, thank you for creating me. I am wonderfully made. I am your creation. I am glad that I never
have to feel worthless, broken, or lonely. I am always
encouraged when I stay in your Word. I pray that you
would continually encourage my heart. I also pray
that you would teach me to encourage myself when
there's only discouragement around me. I trust you
to make good on all that you've promised. I love you.
In Jesus' name. Amen.

Reflection

_____

_____

_____

_____

_____

BE MY FATHER

"Do not be afraid, little flock, for your father
has been pleased to give you the kingdom."
(Luke 12:32)

What do you think when you hear the word,
"father?" Does it conjure up thoughts of being loved
and cared for? Does it bring back memories of good
times? Does it leave you with a smile on your face?
Or, does it bring up painful feelings? Perhaps, it
causes a rush of emotions connected to some past
hurt? Or, perhaps, it doesn't register anything in your
mind because you never had a father? Some of our
earthly fathers have been there for their kids. But,
unfortunately a lot of earthly fathers have not been
what their children need. Does this sound familiar
to you?

If so, Jesus Christ wants you to be sure you have
an accurate picture of the word "father." As the Son
of our heavenly Father, Jesus described Him as being
eager to give you His very Kingdom. "My Son what
is mine is yours." (John 16:15) Christ even indicated
that the Father loves you as much as the Father loves
Him. (See John 17:23) "For great is his love toward
[you]." (Psa. 117:2)

If your earthly father did not measure up to the
man you wanted him to be, God the Father wants you
to know that He is the greatest example of a Father
who came to earth in flesh as Jesus Christ. If you
never had a father, God wants you to know that He

loves you more than you realize. (John 3:16) The One who has saved you from all our sins has open arms waiting to have a personal relationship with you. He wants you to cry out "Abba Father" (Rom. 8:15) and walk into His open arms.

Affirmation

Lord, Be My Father:

- So I can be the greatest father to my kids
- When I have backslidden and moved away from you
- Despite the hurt and pain I feel from my past
- Because I never experienced the love of a father
- So I can have an intimate, personal, relationship with you

Meditation Verse

"The Father loves the Son and has placed everything in his hands." (John 3:36)

Discussion Questions

1. Did you grow up without a father? If so, what difficulties did that pose for you? If not, how did your father impact your life? Positively? Negatively? What would you do the same or differently in raising your own children? Explain.

2. How does God show His children love unlike an earthly father? Are there Bible verses that can guide and support your thoughts on this topic?

3. If you grew up without a father or had nega-
    tive experiences, have you ever expressed
    your hurts and pains to anyone? How can
    your perspective change despite those hurts
    and pains? How will you ask God to help you
    change?

Prayer

Abba Father, I cry out to you. You are my father
whether I knew my earthly father or not. I give you
all of my hurts and pains because I know that you are
a God of comfort. You are there for me still when I
move away from you. You are there no matter what I
do. Please give me forgiveness in my heart to release
the one who abandoned or hurt me. I want to be totally
free to love you with all of my heart because you are
my daddy. You love me unconditionally and you will
never leave me or forsake me. You are always with
me. In that I can trust. I love you dad. In Jesus' name.
Amen.

Reflection

_____

_____

_____

_____

_____

LORD, EXALT ME

"No one from the east or the west or from
the desert can exalt a man.
But it is God who judges: He brings one
down, he exalts another." (Psalm 75:6-7)

The world today can be a tough place to live.
Perhaps, you've been one of those people who've
been trampled on by others trying to get ahead. There's
no more obvious place to see this sort of behavior
than in the workplace. People are striving for more
money, promotion, and influence. Competitiveness,
control, and the pursuit of power are increasingly
becoming rampant in a society that is out of control.
This, unfortunately, is one dysfunctional aspect of
the world in which we live.

Fortunately though, you don't have to rely on
the ways of the world. In the world, the person who
gets the highest grades may get the opportunity
to go to the best college or get the best job. In the
workplace, the person who works the hardest often
gets the promotion or most pay. But, you who are in
Christ receive your pay so-to-speak and promotion
from God. In the blink of an eye, God can move you
into a new position that man said you weren't quali-
fied for. In an instant, He can open up doors that
once appeared to be closed. He can set before you
your heart's desires without you having to do any
work at all.

You may have to go through times when you sit and wait on God, but He will exalt you in due season. (Ecc. 3:1) The life of Joseph is a great example of how God works. Do you remember when Joseph was sold into slavery by his brothers? He also had a difficult encounter with Potipher's wife. Additionally, he had to spend time in prison. All of this happened before he was exalted to second in command in Egypt (Gen. 37, 39-41). Joseph had to endure difficulties at the hands of others, but He received his promotion from God. He was exalted in God's perfect timing.

You must be diligent to work hard in school or at work. God wants you to be excellent in everything you do. He wants you to seek excellence as a student. He wants you to be an excellent employee at work. But, you must not rely on the ways of the world to get ahead. You must rest in Him knowing that your promotion shall come, but you must wait patiently for Him. (Psa. 40:2)

Affirmation

Lord, Exalt Me:
- As I sit still and wait patiently for you
- That your name would be glorified in heaven
- So that others might see and glorify your name
- As an example of your power and might
- So that others would receive salvation

Meditation Verse

"For whoever exalts himself will be humbled, and whoever humbles himself will be exalted." (Matt. 23:12)

Discussion Questions

1. What are some goals you've set for your life? How will you reach your goals? What are your personal strategies? Spiritual strategies? Have you shared your plans with anyone?

2. How does your life plan differ from God's plan for your life? Explain.

3. You probably have received some sort of promotion or raise at some point in life. Has God ever exalted you without you having to put forth any effort? Share with someone or in a small group.

Prayer

Father, my eyes look to the hills to see where my help comes from and it comes from you Lord. I will not turn my eyes away to any other person or thing. For you are the King of kings and Lord of lords. You are marvelous, magnificent, and majestic. Holy is He who sits at the right hand of the Father. I wait for you to exalt me in your perfect timing. You and you alone are worthy of all praise. May your will be done on earth as it is in heaven. In Jesus' name. Amen.

Reflection

_____

_____

_____

_____

_____

HELP ME GUARD MY MOUTH

"He who guards his mouth and his tongue
keeps himself from calamity."
Proverbs 21:23

Have you ever found yourself saying, "I can't believe I said that!" At times, you can find yourself saying things you wish you never said in the first place. The unfortunate thing about words is that once the words are spoken you can't take them back. This can be especially problematic when the words you choose are hurtful to others. If only you had a shy or quiet temperament. If that were the case, perhaps, you would be more apt to keep your mouth shut. But no matter the case, the bottom line is the necessity to think before speaking.

Before you speak, ask yourself, "Will my words be harmful or hurtful?" Ask yourself if a person were to speak the same things about you would the words be true? Will your words build someone up or tear someone down? Will your words be positive and uplifting or is it depressing and inflating? These are important questions to consider before you speak.

The Bible tells us to keep the tongue from evil. (Psa. 34:13) He whose tongue is deceitful falls (17:20) and a lying tongue hates those it hurts. (26:2) But, he who holds his tongue is wise (10:19) and the tongue of the wise brings healing. (12:18) The Bible also tells us that the "tongue is a fire" that has the potential to corrupt a person. Therefore, you must choose your words wisely. (James 3:6) Sometimes, the best thing to do is to leave negative words unspoken. As you may have heard growing up, "If you don't have anything nice to say, then don't say anything."

Affirmation

Help Me Guard My Mouth:

- When I am tempted to say something negative
- When circumstances become stressful
- So I might build up others around me
- During a disagreement with my spouse
- So I can glorify your holy name

Meditation Verse

"For out of the overflow of his heart his mouth speaks." (Luke 6:45)

Discussion Questions

1. Have you every misspoken? Did you say something you regretted and can never take back? Spoken hurtful words to someone? If so, what would you do differently given a second chance? Explain.
2. What does the Bible say about guarding your mouth? Your tongue? Select several verses from your concordance. How do you interpret those verses?
3. Think about different ways you can build up others with your words. Share with someone or in a small group. How can you be mindful to speak positive words everyday?

Prayer

Father, I pray that I would not speak harmful or hurtful words to anyone. Please forgive me if I've ever grieved the Holy Spirit with inappropriate words. I want to be a blessing to others, not a detractor or distracter. I desire to speak words of life, not death. I pray that your Holy Spirit would fill me more each and every day. Help me guard my mouth so that I always glorify your name. In Jesus' name. Amen.

Reflection

_____

_____

_____

_____

_____

HELP ME OVERCOME GUILT

"And having disarmed the powers and
authorities, he made a public spectacle of
them, triumphing over them by the cross."
(Colossians 2:15)

Have you ever talked to yourself? Self-talk can
be affirming and positive. It can also be negative
and disheartening. Chances are that because you are
aware of your own insecurities, you have had some
conversations that were not encouraging. You can be
very hard on yourself when things go wrong. Guilt is
horrible and overcoming it is difficult. The devil uses
it to bring you down so you aren't any good for yourself or others. Not only do we gain a sense of guilt,
but we fully buy into that that's how you should feel,
and the devil totally exploits that emotion.

So, how can you overcome feelings of guilt? Well,
it's a process to be sure. First, acknowledge negative self talk. "What I am saying to myself is negative." Second, change your mind by telling yourself
positive words. "The Truth shall set you free." (John
8:32) Third, allow the Holy Spirit to displace negative
words with positive ones. And, fourth, and finally, set
in your mind to believe God's word over any negative thought that might try to enter your mind.

The right talk is to tell yourself you are forgiven.
Tell yourself you are loved. Tell yourself that every-
thing will be alright because God is on your side.
Because if God be for you who can be against you.

God doesn't want you feeling disheartened in any way. He wants you to experience the affirmation of His love. Do you need to speak with Him today? Why don't you speak to Him right now? He has made you an over comer!

Affirmation

Lord, Help Me Overcome Guilt:
- Because guilt does not come from you
- Through marrying Scripture to my mind
- So that the devil doesn't hold me down
- When I have fallen short of your glory
- Through the help of the Holy Spirit

Meditation Verse

"[L]et us draw near to God with a sincere heart in full assurance of faith, having our hearts sprinkled to cleanse us from a guilty conscience..." (Heb. 10:22)

Discussion Questions

1. Are you feeling guilty or shameful about something? Have you shared it with anyone? Are you ready to share with someone? If so, share with an individual or in a small group.

2. How do you overcome the feeling of guilt when it enters your mind? Do talk to yourself? Exercise? Read the Bible? Explain.

3. Find some scripture verses that encourage you? Does the Bible contain passages about overcoming guilt? If so, which ones? Locate relevant passages and meditate on them.

Prayer

Lord, I enter your presence knowing that you have made me an over comer. I realize that it's not by my strength or might, but your strength and might alone. I put all my trust in your Holy Spirit to guide me. I am grateful that I can overcome because guilt is not of your nature. You are pure love and I taste your sweet fragrance on my lips. I pray that you would direct me when feelings of guilt enter into my mind. I don't want to fall short of your glory. In Jesus' name. Amen.

Reflection

_____

_____

_____

_____

_____

MAKE YOUR SALVATION KNOWN

"He went out and began to talk freely,
spreading the news. As a result, people came
to him from everywhere." (Mark 1:45)

Have you watched the news recently? There's often a lot of bad news. Mass layoffs, rising gas and oil prices, corporate scandals, people committing crimes, etc. People tune in to all channels to hear what's happening. People also share the stories with others and tell them what they heard. The stories are neither good nor uplifting. To the contrary, a lot of news is rather sad and depressing. This begs the question, "Shouldn't we focus on spreading good news?"

Well, that's what the Bible is all about. Remember when Jesus healed the leprous man. Jesus asked the man not to tell others because he did not want people to recognize him. This prohibited him from moving freely from city to city. But, the man was so overjoyed he shared the good news to everyone. As a result, people sought Jesus out wherever he went. The good news spread quickly and touched many lives.

God wants you to share His good news. What has he done in your life? He has not saved you for yourself, but rather so that you might share His love with others. How has he worked in your life? Has He freed you from an addiction? Has He delivered you from lying, cheating, or stealing? Has He saved a non-believing relative or friend? Has He restored you from a broken relationship? Has He guided your prodigal son back home? Perhaps, He has just healed you from a bad cold?

Whatever He has done for you, you should testify so that He will be glorified. What God has done is not just for you. It's so that others will be blessed. God will make His salvation known to all through you. Do you have a testimony?

Affirmation

Lord, Make Your Salvation Known:
- While the pastor preaches on Sunday
- As I live my life surrendered to you
- To my unsaved friends and relatives
- As I overcome my gambling addiction
- So others will be saved and come to faith

Meditation Verse

"Sing to the Lord, all the earth; proclaim his salvation day after day." (1 Ch. 16:23)

Discussion Questions

1. Have you ever shared the gospel with someone? What is your evangelism style? Have you ever guided someone to faith in Christ? Is sharing the good news of Jesus Christ easy or difficult for you? Explain.
2. How has God used you to make His salvation known to someone? Do you have a recent testimony? Share with someone or in a small group.

3. Have you accepted Jesus into your heart? Do you believe he died on the cross for all of your sins? Have you confessed that you are a sinner in need of God's wonderful grace? If you answered, "Yes," to all three questions, then you are now a born again believer who God can use to make His salvation known.

Prayer

Father, I pray that your name would be made known all over the earth. Many people are hungry for something good. I am thankful that sharing the good news of Jesus' death on the cross is the good news that people need to hear. I pray that they would open their heart and mind to be ready to receive you. You have made yourself known to all men so we would be without excuse. I pray that you would draw all men unto yourself. In Jesus' name. Amen.

Reflection

_____

_____

_____

_____

_____

I WANT TO KNOW YOUR VOICE

"His sheep follow him because they know his voice. But they will never follow a stranger; in fact, they will run away from him because they do not recognize a stranger's voice." (John 10:4-5)

Many parents talk to a baby while s/he is still in the womb. You know why? Because the baby is learning to hear its parent's voice early on. The baby hears a variety of sounds in the mother's womb. Some of those sounds are the voice of the baby's parents. When that same baby is born, s/he will turn its head to look when hearing mom or dad speak. The baby remembered the familiar sounds s/he heard early on.

The same is true in our relationship with our Heavenly Father. He is the Great and Mighty God and we are His sheep. You've heard His voice before we ever knew who was speaking. You knew it before you were conceived. He said, "I am the good shepherd; I know my sheep and my sheep know me." (John 10:14) You knew of God because God has made Himself known to you. We have been aware of Him through creation. (See Genesis) God has revealed Himself through the sun, moon, stars, birds, bees, trees, and so much more. (Ibid) And, once you hear His voice, He opens the gate, calls you by name, leads you out, and goes ahead of you so you can follow Him. (John 10:3-4)

Do you recognize when God speaks to you? Have you heard His voice? Many people probably don't spend enough time with God to really recognize His voice and know when He is speaking. He has revealed Himself, but can you hear Him when he is speaking? Like a child, you want to be able to look to God and say, "Father, I hear you speaking and I am listening." For He is the gate and every man who enters through Jesus Christ will be saved. (Mark 10:9)

Affirmation

Lord, I Want to Know Your Voice:

- So that I might receive a Word from you
- To avoid the temptations of the world
- So that I might discern what is right and wrong
- To guide me through difficult situations
- So that I may have a personal relationship with you

Meditation Verse

"...love the Lord your God, listen to his voice, and hold fast to him. For the Lord is your life, and he will give you many years in the land..." (Deut. 30:20)

Discussion Questions

1. Do you know God's voice? How does He speak to you? Through your spouse? During prayer? While reading the Bible? Other?

2. Do you have a testimonial you could share about a time when God spoke to you, how you followed His instruction, and how what He said came true? Share with a friend or in a small group.

3. What do you need to do to get to know God's voice better?

Prayer

Lord, I pray that I might hear a word from you. I want you to speak to me. I desire to know your voice. At times, I feel all alone in this big world, but I know you are always with me. You reside in me. We walk together everyday. You take all of my fears away. You are there when I am tempted. You are there when I struggle. You are there when I am angry, depressed, or simply want to quit. I pray that I might receive a Word from you. Praise to your name. Amen.

Reflection

_____

_____

_____

_____

_____

BLESS YOUR NAME

"I will bless the Lord at all times; His praise
shall continually be in my mouth."
(Psalm 34:1)

Praise you Lord for your splendor and might. Bless your name because you are simply awesome. Praise you for my car, home, spouse, children, money, and everything you provide. Bless your name because you are Jehovah Jireh my provider. Praise you Lord for the invisible things too. Bless your name for the character, integrity, self-control and self-discipline you instill in me. Praise you for your glory, splendor, and overwhelming goodness. You are to be worshipped and exalted.

If you haven't realized it already, heaven is going to be an awesome place one day. Imagine worshipping God full-time. That's all you will do. You will walk around singing and dancing. You will celebrate with the angels and rejoice about how good God is. You will spend all of our time praising, blessing, lifting up, and exalting His name. Your job will be to worship the Lord God almighty!

Well, you can certainly get a foretaste of what that will be like right here on earth. Every time you open your mouth, you can bless His name. Every day you are alive there's a reason to praise Him. Just look outside – the flowers, trees, birds, bees, sky, mountains, sun, moon, stars, and all of His creation. The list of things you can praise Him for is endless because God is infinite. Living a life of praise is blessing the Lord at all times; the praises continually flowing from your lips.

Why not experience heaven everyday? Praise Him and bless His name. He is marvelous. He is wonderful. He is worthy of all praise. Won't you lift your voice and bless Him today?

Affirmation

Father, Bless Your Name:

- Because you are worthy of all praise
- Because your praises are sung without ceasing
- Because you've given me breath in my body
- Because of all the beauty you've created
- Because you are my Father in heaven

Meditation Verse

"…the same Lord is Lord of all and richly blesses all who call on him." (Rom. 10:12)

Discussion Questions

1. How much time do you spend praising God during a day? Week? Should you give God more time? If so, when and how?
2. What does it mean to praise God continually? Is it possible to do so?
3. What do you believe heaven will look like when you get there? How can you create that same picture here on earth?

Prayer

I will bless the Lord at all times. His praises shall continually be in my mouth. I will praise Him in the morning when I rise, at mid-day, and at night before I go to sleep. God is glorious and worthy of all of our praise. I love you Father with all of my heart. Every waking moment I dedicate to serving you. Bless you now in Jesus' name. Amen.

Reflection

_____

_____

_____

_____

_____

YOU ARE MY SUPPLIER

"God shall supply all of your needs
according to His riches and glory in Christ
Jesus." (Philippians 4:19)

Think about your life? What do you need right now? Are you experiencing a broken family relationship? Are you stuck in a bad financial situation? Are you unemployed seeking a job? Are you ill at home or in the hospital trying to get better? Are you feeling spiritually empty, perhaps, ready to give up?

Well, if any of the above-mentioned questions rings your bell, you probably could go to a specialist (e.g., a counselor, financial specialist, or doctor) to get some help. But, who could you call if you had multiple issues. You wouldn't call the doctor to help with financial issues. You wouldn't call a financial specialist to help with medical issues. You could, however, call on God and He could provide for all of your needs because He is Jehovah Jireh your sole provider.

God will meet you at the point of your need based on His goodness alone. When it comes to God, it's not about who you know or how much money you have. It's not about who you rub shoulders with or what your resume looks like. It's not about how wealthy your family is or the zip code where you reside. No, it's not about any of those things. The Lord dispenses to you His riches and glory in Christ Jesus who shall supply all of your needs. (Phil. 4:19)

God doesn't want you to be lacking anything. He desires to meet you right where you are. He wants to provide for all, not just some, of your needs. He is a supplier of your needs so that you may always be ready to be an encouragement to others. He is the supplier of all of your needs so that you may always be ready to give Him glory. Why not trust Him for what you need right now?

Affirmation

Jehovah, You Are My Supplier:

- When I have been laid off from my job
- When I am not in the right state of mind
- When I am struggling to overcome an addiction
- When I am experiencing problems in my marriage
- When I am feeling spiritually empty

Meditation Verse

"When I said, 'My foot is slipping,' your love, Oh Lord, supported me." (Psalm 94:18)

Discussion Questions

1. What current need(s) do you have in your life? Emotional? Financial? Physical? Other? Have you asked God to help you meet your need(s)? If yes, share your testimony. If no, share your situation with someone or in a small group.
2. Do you have a testimonial about how the Lord met an important need in your life? Share it

with a friend or in a small group? What was the result of God meeting your need? Has your view of God changed? Has your faith increased? Explain.

3. Does God really supply all of our needs? How do you interpret Philippians 4:19? Should we interpret the verse literally? Explain.

Prayer

Father, I come humbly before you. I recognize that you are the one true God who can provide for my every need. I thank you that you meet me right where I am. Thank you for not leaving me or forsaking me at any moment. I pray for all the needs that I have right now. I pray that you would help me get through my struggles. You know every detail of my situation. I trust you. In Jesus' name I pray. Amen.

Reflection

_____

_____

_____

_____

_____

WORKING WITH PURPOSE

"Always give yourselves fully to the work of
the Lord, because you know that your labor
in the Lord is not in vain." (1 Cor. 15:58)

Have you ever been dissatisfied or unhappy on the job? Sometimes problems arise in the workplace as a result of some action or inaction of the employer or employee. The workplace can be a miserable place at times for any number of reasons. You can contribute to your relative dissatisfaction based on your attitude. Or, you can adopt a positive attitude, which can change the environment and your outlook.

God has given you the skill and ability to rise above the place where you are. "We are more than conquers." (Rom. 8: 37) God wants us to maximize our potential through the power He's given us. You cannot give your best if you choose to sulk and wallow in a pit of unhappiness. You must realize that you are not working for the company. You are working for God. "Always give yourselves fully to the work of the Lord, because you know that your labor in the Lord is not in vain." (1 Cor. 15:58)

God has made every individual in a unique way. He has given you have special talents, knowledge, skills, and gifts that are unique to who you are. God knew in the beginning what work He prepared for you to do. "For we are God's workmanship, created in Christ Jesus to do good works, which God prepared in advance for us to do." (Eph. 2:10)

"I know that there is nothing better for men than to be happy and do good while they live. That everyone may eat and drink, and find satisfaction in all his toil – This is the gift of God." (Ecc. 3:12-13) Have you fully committed yourself to work for the Lord? Do you serve God or man in the workplace? If you've chosen the latter, isn't it time you changed your focus? Isn't it time you worked with a greater purpose in mind?

Affirmation

Lord, I desire to Work with Purpose:
- When I am working under little supervision
- When I feel unhappy or dissatisfied
- When I am frustrated with my supervisor
- When I am feeling unproductive
- Because ultimately you are my boss

Meditation Verse

"The sluggard craves and gets nothing, but the desires of the diligent are fully satisfied." (Proverbs 13:4)

Discussion Questions

1. Are you a diligent worker or a sluggard on the job? If you are diligent do you know someone who wastes time? How does that make you feel? If you waste too much time or are slothful, how can you change in light of Proverbs 13:4? Explain.
2. Was Jesus' life an example of diligent work? If so, how? If not, why not? Explain and

provide biblical evidence to support your assertion.

3. How can you be an example to others to help avoid wasting time at work? What actions can you take?

Prayer

Lord, you created me in your likeness. You have made me unique in my talents, gifts, skills, and abilities. You want me to use all of who I am to be a blessing to others. I pray that you would give me the wisdom to do good and not waste time. Every waking moment counts and every moment I waste impacts your kingdom. Make me diligent everyday so that others would see the work of my hands and glorify the Father in heaven. In Jesus' name. Amen.

Reflection

_____

_____

_____

_____

_____

WALKING IN YOUR WAYS

"The ways of the Lord are right; the righteous walk in them." (Hosea 14:9)

Have you noticed how much stock people put into other people and things? You hear a news report about something on television and you immediately take it as factual. After all, it's the news and it must be true, right? You gasp at some headline-catching story that intrigues you. Yet, you haven't heard all the facts to actually determine whether what you've heard is true. You invest in the stock market and make other investments to build quick capital despite market uncertainty. You shutter when the market collapse and prices take a dive. You put your trust in people, cars, homes, etc. trusting that these things will make you happy and give you a better life. It's only when the things fail do we realize that we haven't put our trust in the right place.

Thankfully, you can place your trust in God. "Those who know [His] name will trust." (Psa. 9:10) and do good. (Psa. 37:3) You can trust all of his statutes. His living Word will never fail you. Therefore, you ought to do His will and follow Him because "all His precepts are trustworthy." (Psa. 111:7) Thus, unlike the things of the world, you need not worry about things changing when it comes to the Word. God is the same yesterday, today, and forevermore. (Heb. 13:8) When you follow His ways, you are certainly doing the right thing. "The righteous shall live by faith" (Gal. 3:11).

Are you walking in the ways of the Lord or the world? The Bible reads: "Do not conform to the pattern of this world, but be transformed by the renewing of your mind." (Rom. 12:2) Do you need to get rid of some areas of 'stinking thinking' in your life? Do you need more certainty rather than uncertain worldly things? If so, "show love for the Lord by walking according to His statutes." (I Kings 3:3)

Affirmation

I am Walking In Your Ways:
- Because I want to love you with all of my heart
- As the leader of my household
- Despite the temptations and lure of the world
- Because I desire to be obedient to you
- So that I may agape you everyday of my life

Meditation Verse

"As for God, his way is perfect; the word of the Lord is flawless." (2 Sam. 22:31)

Discussion Questions

1. How is your walk with the Lord? Are you surrendered to Him in every area of your life? If not, what area(s) do you need to surrender? Be honest and examine yourself.

2. What tempts you? What are your areas of weakness? How do you avoid being lured

into sin? Are there passages in the Bible that address temptation and how you can avoid it? If so, how can you apply those passages to your life?

3. What things have your placed your trust in? What do you need to do to remove those things that you have put before God? What do you need to stop doing so that God will be first in your life?

Prayer

Father, I choose to follow you in the morning, noon, and night. I know that it is futile putting my trust in the things of the world. So, I choose to walk in your ways. I cannot trust in my home, car, job, or any material things. I cannot trust man either. People and things won't last, but your Word endures forever. I wish to be obedient to all of your statutes. This day, I choose to follow you for it is right for me to do so. In Jesus' name. Amen.

Reflection

_____

_____

_____

_____

_____

LET ME DO GOOD

"As you have done, it will be done to you;
your deeds will return upon your own head."
(Obadiah 15)

When you think about good deeds what comes to mind? Helping an old lady across the street? Opening a door for someone as they approach an entrance? Yielding to someone on the highway when that person needs to stop, pull over, or change lanes. Helping someone get up when they've fallen down? Well, all of these acts are great examples of doing good for others. Oprah Winfrey might describe these acts as "random acts of kindness." Doing good things for people so that doing good becomes contagious and encourages others to do good too.

In the story of the Good Samaritan, the priest and Levite had an opportunity to help a man who fell into the hands of robbers. But, they passed him by. The Samaritan, however, took pity on the man. He went to him and bandaged his wounds. He then put the man on his donkey and took him to an inn to care for him. (Luke 10:25-37) The Samaritan didn't have to stop and help. He wasn't legally obligated to do so. But, he did nevertheless.

God wants us to totally devote our lives to Him. We can do this by showing love through our actions. The Bible says, "The only thing that counts is faith expressing itself through love." (Gal. 5:6) Jesus wants you to "love the Lord [ ] God with all your

197

heart and with all your soul and with all your strength and with all your mind, and love your neighbor as yourself." (Luke 10:27) You can show your love for God by doing good deeds.

If you follow the teachings of Christ, the blessings of your actions will flow back to you. "Let us do evil that good may result?" (Rom. 3:8) No, of course not! "Love does not delight in evil." (I Cor. 13:6) Rather, "I have the desire to do what is good," (Rom. 7:18), because God is good so "as [you] have opportunity, [] do good." (Gal. 6:10)

Affirmation

Lord, Let Me Do Good:
- When others try to influence me negatively
- By remaining faithful to the truth of the Word
- Because you want me to imitate Christ Jesus
- So that others can see the goodness in me
- When I am confronted with evil circumstances

Meditation Verse

A good man leaves an inheritance for his children's children." (Prov. 13:22)

Discussion Questions

1. What do you think about when you consider 'random acts of kindness?' Are these acts something you should do randomly or regularly? What kind of act(s) have you done recently for someone? Explain.

2. Have you ever failed to act or do something good for someone when you had the chance to do so? If so, do you regret your decision? How would you respond differently if you had the opportunity to do it over again?

3. How can you experience more of God's goodness everyday? How can you live in such a way to make doing good contagious and infect others?

Prayer

Lord, you are good to me. You are better to me than I realize. I want to taste and see how good you are. I want to know more about you so I can go higher in your glory. Your Word tells me that I am to be an imitator of your son, Jesus Christ. I need your strength to help me walk with you everyday. It's only because you are good that I have the opportunity to be good. I pray that you would show me what it means to be a true son of God. In Jesus' name. Amen.

Reflection

_____

_____

_____

_____

_____

GOD IS WATCHING

"Surely the eyes of the Sovereign Lord are
on the sinful kingdom." (Amos 9:8)

Do you remember when you were a child and you
did some things you thought no one would ever find
out about? Maybe it was taking candy from the store.
Maybe you took a crayon and wrote all over your
bedroom wall. You did something you knew you
shouldn't be doing, but you thought no one would be
the wiser. Eventually, someone discovered what you
did and you got into trouble. Well, as adults, we do
some of the same things, but in even more harmful
ways; with even greater consequences.

Maybe you had an affair with someone who was
not your wife. Maybe you watched pornography
on the Internet at your office or home. Maybe you
engaged in a perverted act or other sexually deviant
activity when no one else was around. The consequences of your actions, perhaps, led to a broken
marriage, sexually transmitted disease, jail or something worse. And, you thought no one was watching
you? Well, even if no human saw what you did, you
always get caught because God is always watching.
(Psa. 145:20)

God sees the good we do, but he also watches
the wickedness. "Does He who formed the eye
not see?" (Psa. 94:9) Surely, He watches every act
of man whether it be good or bad. He is the "God
who judges the earth." (Psa. 58:11) Therefore, you

ought to always do that which is right in the sight of the Lord because even when you think no one is watching, the Lord sees you.

Are there areas of your life that you know are not God's will for you? Do you have some sin that you are hiding from others? God is watching your every move. He knows everything you do or fail to do to please Him. There's nowhere to run or hide. Why don't you just surrender all to Him today?

Affirmation

God Is Watching:

- So that I might be without stain or blemish
- So I would be a light at home and work
- When I am alone and no one else is watching
- So I will be a good leader for my family
- Because He loves and cares for His children

Meditation Verse

The "eyes of the Lord are continually [watching] from the beginning of the year to its end." (Deut. 11:12)

Discussion Questions

1. Think about one thing you've done in private (when no one else was around) that you are ashamed of? Have you asked God for forgiveness? Are you still tormented by it today? Have you healed? Share with someone or in a small group.

2. Is there some sin in your life right now that you have not dealt with? Aren't you tired of keeping secrets? Telling lies? Cheating? Cutting corners? Trying to cover up your wrongs? Be honest with yourself.

3. Take some time to pray about the area(s) where you are falling short. Ask God to bring conviction into your life so you can 'cut it out.' Ask Him to guide you to repentance so you would do an about face on your sin and never look back again. Are you ready to end the charade and turn to a new chapter? God is watching!

Prayer

I pray for conviction in the area(s) of my life that are outside of your will. I pray that you would lead me down a path of righteousness. I desire to be pure in heart at home with my family, on the job with co-workers, and in my local community. You want me to be a light to others. You are always watching so I want to be pleasing to you every moment of everyday. Teach me your ways. In Jesus' name. Amen.

Reflection

_____

_____

_____

_____

_____

I WAIT FOR YOU

"But as for me, I watch in hope for the Lord,
I wait for God my Savior; my God will hear
me." (Micah 7:7)

One thing many people don't like to do is wait. Society today is filled with impatient people. People don't like standing in line for too long at the store. People get frustrated when the stoplight isn't turning green fast enough. People must be served in a restaurant in a timely manner or else there's a big fuss. "I want it right now" is the attitude toward many things in life. People don't like to wait.

How God operates though is often very different from what we want. God is not in a rush. He doesn't see time like we see time. For us a few minutes may seem like an eternity. Wait? Why wait? We say, "Open up another line!" Our thought eventually shifts to moving someone out of our way, causing a commotion because we have to wait longer than we want, or doing whatever we must to get what we want – no matter the cost to others.

The Bible says, "be not anxious for anything, but in everything, by prayer and petition, with thanksgiving, present your requests to God." (Phil. 4:6) God doesn't want you to entertain self-condemned, worry. Rather, you are to trust Him in everything and wait patiently on Him. When you try to go ahead of or against God it's always counter-productive. You always get results that are less than what God can get for you.

God wants you to learn to wait and be more patient in life. He guides you down this path because He already knows the benefit of us waiting. He has a plan for you. (Jer. 29:11) He may have a lesson He wants you to learn. He may have something better for you if you would just wait a little longer. He may want to teach you to have more patience. He may try to show you that it's simply not the right season for you to move. He may want you to learn to trust Him more.

Are you worried about something? Are you thinking about moving out on your own? Has God given you instruction to move out? If not, will you trust Him by waiting on His instruction and perfect timing? You will be glad you waited.

Affirmation

Lord, I Wait For You:

- Because I am tired of doing things my way
- While I stand in a long line at the grocery store
- When the stoplight is red and I am late for work
- While I am incarcerated waiting to be released
- Because you are my Rock and my Redeemer

Meditation Verse

"I waited patiently for the Lord." (Psalms 40:1)

Discussion Questions

1. Think about a time when you had to wait a long time and you got a bad attitude? What did you do or say that was inappropriate? Ungodly? How would you respond differently today?

2. In what area(s) of your life do you need to be more patient? Is patience connected with faith in some way? If so, how can you work to get better in areas where you are impatient?

3. Using the concordance in your Bible, look up the word 'wait' and review the relevant Scripture verses associated with that word. Interpret the relevant verses and answer the following question: What does God mean when he asks you to wait?

Prayer

Lord God, teach me to patiently wait on you. Teach me not to go ahead of or against you, but rather to wait on your perfect timing. I would rather be one who was sent rather than one who went. I realize that the results of moving out on my own can be disastrous. True success comes through doing things according to your will. I wait on you Almighty God for how perfect your love is. Blessed be your name. Amen.

Reflection

_____

_____

_____

_____

_____

I Trust In You

"The Lord is good, a refuge in times of trouble.
He cares for those who trust in him." (Nahum 1:7)

September 2008 was one of the toughest periods in the history of the United States. The country was at war in Iraq and Afghanistan, struggling against threats of terrorism from other countries, hit with a recession, watching financial markets and businesses tumble to lows like never before, and shifting presidential leadership. All the instability led to massive lay-offs, bankruptcy filings by individuals and businesses, scarcity of homes, casualties of war (loss of life), and relative uncertainty for all in everyday life.

The one constant in uncertainty is God. The Lord never changes. He is the same yesterday, today, and forevermore (Heb. 13:8). Psalm 91 reads: "I will say of the Lord, He is my refuge and my fortress, my God in whom I trust" (91:2). Fortunately, God is not like a wave in the ocean tossed back and forth. He is not like a shifting shadow on a sunny day. He is not volatile like the stock market. No, the Lord is constant, consistent, and steady. He doesn't change. He remains constant everyday. (Heb. 13:8)

God wants you to trust Him despite how unfavorable things might appear. If you can't pay your mortgage, trust Him. If you lost someone due to war, trust Him. If your 401k and investments are upside down, trust Him. If you have to file for bankruptcy, you're deep in debt, or facing other circumstances that seem insurmountable, trust Him. "And, we know that in all things God works for the good of those who have been called according to his purpose." (Rom. 8:28) He can do immeasurably more than we can ask or think. (Eph. 3:20)

Affirmation

God, I Trust in You:

- In the midst of my unemployment
- Despite the loss of a loved one
- To help me dig out of a mountain of debt
- Because I know you care for me
- For you are my shelter in times of trouble

Meditation Verse

"Those who know your name will trust in you, for you, Lord, have never forsaken those who seek you." (Psalm 9:10)

Discussion Questions

1. What are you going through right now? What challenges are you facing? Are you unemployed? Have you recently lost a loved one? How are you handling your circumstances? How do you trust God despite your situation?

2. Do you trust God to get you through tough times? Read Psalm 91 and meditate on that passage. Review other Bible verses that emphasize trusting God.

3. In what area of your life do you need to trust God more? In the area(s) you
4. identified can you determine what's stopping you from trusting Him completely?

Prayer

Father, it makes my life easier when I trust you. I trust you during times of unemployment, financial hardship, the loss of a loved one, when I am sinking in debt, and when my marriage or relationship isn't working. I don't have to worry about controlling anything because you are in control. I don't have worry about meeting any needs because you are Jehovah Jireh my provider. I don't have to worry whether things will be alright because you are a great and mighty God. Bless your name. Amen.

Reflection

_____

_____

_____

_____

_____

HELP ME HEAL HEARTS

"I tell you the truth, whatever you did for
one of the least of these brothers of mine,
you did for me." (Matthew 25:40)

Some of the most rewarding work in life occurs when you can help individuals who are hungry, thirsty, lonely, or with other needs. There is tremendous gratification in serving others. But, there is often more to helping others than meets the eye. We learn this when Jesus' disciples questioned him about eternal life and the end of the world. He answered their questions with a series of parables, concluding with one about sheep and goats. (See Matt. 25:31) In it, the Son of Man condemned the goats for not meeting needs of those who needed it most. On the other hand, He commended the sheep for doing what the goats did not, and they were surprised by their reward.

The words of Matthew 25:40 give us some insight. When we reach out to help one of God's children in need, we actually minister to God Himself. The parable is a dialogue between God and the nations of the world, not these already following Him. That's why the sheep were amazed. They did recognize Jesus as the significance of their actions. They weren't acting out of desire for reward, but rather were serving sacrificially without any need of recognition. They were imitating Christ's sacrificial love

210

for people while simultaneously teaching believers who already know God.

This parable is an excellent reminder of how eternally significant is every act of love. When we help with the right heart, we not only help others, but we glorify God and move forward His kingdom agenda. The parable assumes that those who follow God will automatically treat others as Jesus did. But, experience shows this will not always be the case. When we need to be reminded, we can reflect on this parable. We are called to be a sheep, not only saved, but motivated to carry out God's purpose and plan.

Affirmation

God, Help Me Heal Hearts:
- To model your love for those who don't know you
- Without self-ambition or vain conceit
- So that I might minister to other believers
- So that I might glorify the King of kings
- Like a sheep unaware of any reward

Meditation Verse

"Do not forget the helpless." (Psalm 10:12a)

Discussion Questions

1. What do you do to help others in need? Serve at a homeless shelter or in a homeless ministry? Provide food or clothing for those struggling to make ends meet? What other ways do you help?

2. What does the Bible say about helping others in need? Should social justice be part of church-life? Are we obligated to help others? Commanded? Discuss with someone or in a small group.

3. How does helping someone move forward God's kingdom agenda? Explain.

Prayer

Father, I pray that you would give me a compassionate heart for people who don't have as I have. I pray for those who feel left out, sick, shut in, shut out, left behind, and overlooked by our society. You don't want me to forget those without hope. Rather, you want me to model the love you have instilled in me so that others might come to a saving knowledge of you. Help me imitate your son. In Jesus' name. Amen.

Reflection

_____

_____

_____

_____

_____

OPEN MY EYES

"Delight yourself in the Lord and he will
give you the desire of your heart."
(Psalm 37:4)

Psalm 37:4 is an exciting verse in the Bible. It seems to read that if I enjoy God He will give me everything I desire. Wouldn't it great if that were the case? You could get everything you want with the touch of a wand or snap of a finger? Well, the reality is that God doesn't wave a magic wand or is not like a genie in a bottle. You cannot expect Him to instantly give you everything you want. Instead of a promise of prosperity, the passage is filled with words that reflect a profound truth. The closer you draw to Him, the more your desires will reflect His.

The writer of Psalm 37 encourages his readers not to worry in times of trouble, but delight in the Lord. He encourages you to experience ultimate joy and satisfaction, and a rich life. This encouragement is meant to be an ongoing process. You are to delight in God on a daily basis. This means that our desires will be His as you draw closer to Him. This allows you to be aligned with His purpose and plan your life.

How are you delighting yourself in the Lord? Have you been spending enough time with Him? Have you discovered His desires for your heart? Do you know your purpose in life? Have you spent time thanking Him for how He's helping you to grow?

Have you experienced the power of being in His presence? The Bible says, "[L]et us draw near to God." (Heb. 10:22) "[He] will fill [you] with joy in [His] presence." Acts 2:28

Affirmation

Lord, Open My Eyes:
- I want to experience true joy, peace, and happiness
- To help me understand who you are and whose I am
- So my heart will be like your heart everyday
- In fresh, new, ways so I might experience your fullness
- I want to see you, I want to see you

Meditation Verse

"I delight greatly in the Lord." (Isa. 61:10)

Discussion Questions

1. How do you delight in the Lord? How have you been spending your time with Him? Have you been giving God enough time? If not, how can you spend more time with Him? What do you need to do? Share your thoughts with someone or in a small group.

2. What are the desires for your heart? Have you shared them with anyone? What is your purpose in life? Why has God placed you on earth?

3. Have you taken some time to thank God for how He has blessed you? Have you expe-

rienced the power of being in His presence this week? Take some time to pray and give thanks to the Creator of the universe.

Prayer

I come to you on bended knees to worship you, Lord. In your presence, I experience joy, peace, and tranquility. I give my whole heart to you. I want to see you. I want to know you. I desire to be more like you. Open the eyes of my heart. Help me understand whose I am at the deepest level. In Jesus' name. Amen.

Reflection

_____

_____

_____

_____

_____

HEAL MY HEART

"He heals the brokenhearted and binds up
their wounds." (Psalm 147:3)

People hurt from all sorts of wounds. But, there is
no pain like a broken heart. Most people experience
the pain of a break up at least once in their life. Often,
it happens with the very first dating relationship. You
fall head-over-heals for a person who you believe
is your future spouse. You eventually discover that
the relationship won't last and it ends in heartache.
"What am I going to do without her!" You gasp. The
situation makes you feel miserable. Some never get
over the pain and are still hurting today.

Pain can sometimes lead us down the wrong
path. Some turn to drugs or alcohol to mask the pain.
Some hurt the next person they date because of unre-
solved pain. Some set out to conquer as many other
relationships as possible because they feel they can
never trust again. Some simply stop dating altogether
because they never want to experience a broken heart
again. One thing for sure, pain is real.

But, God did not create you so you would be
stuck in your circumstances. He loves you too much
to leave you stuck with a hurting heart. You must
remember that Jesus understands a broken heart.
Imagine the depth of the pain He felt when those He
loved rejected Him. (Mark 8:31) Trust that He knows
what you are going through. He cares, and He is here
to heal you. "Who can heal you?" (Lam. 2:13) Jesus

healed many. (See The Gospels) For He is the Lord who heals you, (Exod. 15:26), He can bind up the wounds of your broken heart. (Ps. 147:3) Why don't you give Him a try? The living God is waiting to remove your pain and heal your heart.

Affirmation

Lord, Heal My Heart:

- Because I long for a deeper relationship with you
- So I can forgive as you have forgiven me
- Because I still hurt from past pain
- When I feel like a failure
- So I don't stay stuck

Meditation Verse

"Heal me, O Lord, and I will be healed." (Jer. 17:14)

Discussion Questions

1. Does God allow us to have a broken heart or is it something that happens because of our own choices? Explain.
2. How do you think Jesus felt when he was betrayed? How do you think he feels when His people break His heart?
3. Are you experiencing heart ache right now? Have you shared your pain with anyone? With God? Are you ready to allow Him to heal you so you can move forward? God is waiting to heal you.

Prayer

Oh God, I pray for your healing power. All I want is a touch from you. When I am hurting, I need your healing power. When I've been offended, I need your healing power. When my heart has been broken, I need your healing power. Help me to forgive the hurt from the past so I can move on to the new things in the future. I pray that you would empower me to trust you more everyday. In Jesus' mighty name. Amen.

Reflection

_____

_____

_____

_____

_____

THE ONE AND ONLY

"The Word became flesh and made his
dwelling among us. We have seen his glory,
the glory of the One and Only, who came
from the Father, full of grace and truth."
(John 1:14)

Have you ever had a surprise party? Have you
ever received a special delivery package you did not
expect? If so, then you can understand the feeling of
utter shock. You didn't even see it coming. Surprise!
You were caught off guard. Nevertheless, it was a
good surprise. One that you will probably not soon
forget. Can you imagine receiving a surprise of
even greater proportion? Well, a lot of us received
a "special delivery" the day God came to earth.
Surprise! God sent His son – a miracle of dynamic
proportions!

John tells us that the Word came in the form of
Jesus Christ and he made His dwelling among us.
(John 1:14) This special delivery came as a celebration and package with important contents. The God
of the universe came to dwell with us so that we could
better understand Him, connect with Him, and experience His goodness. (Ibid) God's Word is the most
intimate and informative means of communication
with those whom He has created. (Heb. 4:12) John
helps his readers understand that there is a connection between Jesus, the Word, and the Creator. (John
1:14) In his life on earth, Jesus was both fully human

and fully God. But, John also informs us that Jesus was sent by the Father to bring grace and truth to me and you. (John 5:37; 1 John 4:14)

Has your special delivery arrived? Do you celebrate the good news of Jesus Christ in your life? If not, it's time to celebrate! "For God so loved the world that He gave His one and only Son, that whoever believes in Him shall not perish but have eternal life." (John 3:16) God sent us the greatest gift of all – His son who forgives sin and saves you from death. Jesus is a gift that will never stop giving. If you are ready to receive Him, open up the package because the contents will set you free and give you a new life. (John 8:36)

Affirmation

God, you are The One and Only:

- Because you are present in my times of trouble
- Because you reach out to help meet all of my needs
- Because you have revealed yourself through your Word
- Because I recognize your humanity and Deity
- Because you sacrificed your son so I might have life

Meditation Verse

"Give thanks to the God of gods." (Psalm 136:2)

Discussion Questions

1. What's really important in life? What should you be doing to make a difference in your life? What did Jesus do to make a difference? Write down your list and share it with someone or in a small group.

2. Think about a time when you received a surprise. Describe the circumstances and explain how it made you feel. Were you shocked? What's the best thing about a surprise? Have you ever surprised someone? How did that person respond?

3. Have you received Jesus Christ as Lord and Savior in your life? Are you ready to do so right now? If so, invite Jesus into your life, believe that he died on the cross, and confess your need for God's grace.

Prayer

Lord, I desire to receive you in my life. I accept that you are the God that I want to serve. I want you to be Lord in my life. I confess that I am a sinner in need of your wonderful grace. I desire your salvation. I believe that your son, Jesus Christ, died on the cross for all of my sins – past, present, and future. I pray that as I receive you that you would bless me in ways I never imagined. In Jesus' name I pray. Amen.

Reflection

_____

_____

_____

_____

_____

HOLY, WHOLLY, HOLY

"May God himself, the God of peace, sanc-
tify you through and through. May your
whole spirit, soul and body be kept blameless at the coming of our Lord Jesus Christ."
(I Thess. 5:23)

Have you ever tried to piece together a jigsaw
puzzle? The puzzle has a lot of parts. All of the
pieces have to be put together in the right place.
When the parts are put together the puzzle is whole
and complete. Then you can see the big picture that
you couldn't see at the outset.

Life is the same way. There are many components
to life: family, job, kids, school, physical health,
emotional stability, hobbies, finances, new and
different experiences, and a relationship with God. In
our day-to-day life things can appear to be disjointed.
Sometimes, things just don't seem to come together.
There are moments when it seems that the parts are
not connected and the puzzle is very complicated.
But, that's contrary to how God has designed things.

God doesn't want you to live a "holey" life – a
life that has disconnected parts. He wants you to be
whole and complete. God wants you to be "holy"
and blameless in his sight. (Eph. 1:4) He wants you
to be sanctified, set apart, and different from those
who don't know Him. (1 Cor. 6:11) In God's plan,
every part of life connects with His loving plan. But,
different than a jigsaw puzzle, we must realize that

we can't be lone rangers. We cannot do it alone. Becoming whole is not achieved by one – meaning you alone. Rather, it's done by the One – through His power. (Luke 1:17; Acts 15:8)

Without Almighty God, you will live a holey life with disconnected parts. But, with Him, you can ask for His help to pull everything together in conformity to His will. As we surrender everything to Him, He allows us to see how everything comes together. Your relationship, job, family, friends, and your dreams are all connected because everything is linked to the Source. Can you see the big picture of what's going on in your life? Have you asked God for help you get a better glimpse of what it is and what it's supposed to look like? There's not a better time than now to ask Him.

Affirmation

Lord, Holy, Wholly, Holy when:
- It seems like my life is spiraling out of control
- Life has no real points of connection
- I am experiencing mid-life crisis
- I am faced with an abrupt lay off at work
- Because you Lord God Almighty are Holy

Meditation Verse

"Holy, holy, holy is the Lord God Almighty, who was, and is, and is to come." (Rev. 4:8)

Discussion Questions

1. Are there areas of your life that seem disconnected? Why are the pieces of the puzzle simply not connecting? How can you change your perspective? What must you do? What will it take?

2. Assess your physical health, work life, family life, etc. How are you doing in these areas? Are things woven together nicely? What would your family, co-workers, boss, or others say about you?

3. Can you see the larger vision of what God has for you? Can you see beyond the enemy's schemes and distractions of this world? Explain.

Prayer

Father, you are a Holy God and you desire that your people live a holy life. When things don't seem to be going right, I must remember that you are holy. When I am feeling fleshly and want to fight. I must remember that you are holy. When my day is going wrong and I am feeling blue, I must remember that you are holy. When I cannot trust anyone, I remember that you are holy. Holy, holy, holy is the Lord God almighty and I worship you. In Jesus' name. Amen.

Reflection

_____

_____

_____

_____

_____

CHANGE MY MIND

"Do not be conformed to the patterns of this
world, but be transformed by the renewing
of your mind, then you will be able to test
and approve what God's will is – His good,
pleasing and perfect will. (Romans 12:2)

Have you ever changed your mind about something? You purchased an item at the store, but you decided to return it and get your money back? Or you were driving in a particular direction to a specific location and you decided to go in a different direction? Your mind is the control central of your thoughts, feelings, actions, and emotions. Before you commit your life to Christ, you make decisions based on your own thoughts. Something in the surrounding culture influences your thinking or causes your opinion to sway. You then decide to think differently or take different action. You think you know what's best.

But, once you invite God into your life, your thoughts are no longer your own. There's a change in influence and direction. When you invite God in, He desires to direct and guide your mind. He provides you with the power to transform your mind, to change the way you think so your mind will be in line with His heart. (Rom. 12:2) God wants to allow your mind to become what he originally intended it to be. God wants you to experience an internal change so you can conform the outer shell of your being to be more like His son, Jesus Christ. (Ibid)

You experience this change by replacing your own thoughts with Godly thoughts. The Bible says, "Whatever is true, whatever is noble, whatever is right, whatever is pure, whatever is lovely, whatever is admirable – if anything is excellent or praise worthy – think about such things. Whatever you have learned … put it into practice. And the God of peace will be with you." (Phil. 4:8) God doesn't want you to remain the same. He wants to guide you to a renewed way of thinking. He wants you to adopt a mind of Christ so you can truly know His will – His good, pleasing, and perfect will. (Rom. 12:2)

Affirmation

Father, Change My Mind:

- When I am thinking impure thoughts
- When I am abusive to my wife and kids
- When I am tempted to so something illegal
- When I am considering abandoning my family
- When I am working to overcome an addiction

Meditation Verse

"Test me, O Lord, and try me, examine my heart and my mind; for your love is ever before me, and I walk continually in your truth." (Psalm 26:2-3)

Discussion Questions

1. Take a moment to reflect on your thought life. Have you confessed your impure thoughts? Do you ever have thoughts of hurting yourself

or others? How can you overcome 'stinking thinking?' What guidance does the Bible provide?

2. Is there some area of your thought life that you know is not fully surrendered to God? Explain. What will it take for you to completely surrender your entire thought life to Him?

3. Read Romans 12:2 to yourself and then meditate on that verse. Identify area(s) you desire to change and ask God specifically to change your mind. Find a Christian brother to hold you accountable.

Prayer

Father, I pray today for complete renewal of my mind. I don't want to remain the same. I desire the change that I know only you can bring. I want you to guide my thoughts. I want you to guide all of my ways. I don't want to think on my own. I want you to think for me – guide my thoughts and lead me to the way everlasting. I pray that you will do permanent damage to my ignorance. Change the way I think so I can go higher in your glory. Thank you in advance for what you're going to do in Jesus' name. Amen.

Reflection

_____

_____

_____

_____

_____

SHOW ME YOUR SUCCESS

"Do not let this Book of the Law depart
from your mouth; meditate on it day and
night, so that you may be careful to do
everything written in it. Then you will be
prosperous and successful. (Joshua 1:8)

Do you have any wealthy friends? Have you ever seen or heard of someone who is living a wealthy lifestyle? Perhaps, in real life or on television? A business man, professional athlete, or other individual. They seem to have everything going for them. They make a lot of money, drive a fancy car, live in a big house, etc. They seem to have discovered the secret to success, right?

Well, success in the world is different than God's formula for success. Success in the world is often measured by what we have, how much we have, and the path that leads us there. God's formula for success is different. God shared His secret for future success with Joshua after Moses died. You remember the story when Joshua took over for Moses to lead the Israelites into the Promised Land. (Joshua 1:8) God didn't offer Joshua any military insight (i.e., tips) or promise any special powers. He simply reminded him to let the Word influence his life. (Ibid) He simply encouraged Joshua to study the Scriptures. (Ibid) God desired that His Word would anchor itself in his life by soaking into his mind and daily being applied in his life.

God's recipe for success is clearly distinct from the world's definition. The results are distinct too. God doesn't promise that you will instantly have a lot of money, a big house, a fancy car, or happiness as a reward for living right. He does say, however, that if you get to know him better through the Bible, then you will prosper and be successful. You will be fulfilling a unique role He has set aside for you in this world. God is promising you riches that are invisible now, but one day will be revealed to you. His treasures in heaven await you.

Affirmation

Lord, Show Me Your Success:
- Despite how the world defines it
- Even when my marriage isn't going well
- Even when I am not satisfied with the things I have
- Even when my house, car, and job are not fulfilling
- Even when I want to do things a different way

Meditation Verse

"But seek first His kingdom and His righteousness and all these things will be given to you as well." (Matthew 6:33)

Discussion Questions

1. What is your greatest accomplishment in life? How did you achieve it? What was the end result? Was it successful in the eyes of man or God?
2. Do you find fulfillment in your work, home, family life? If so, what do you find fulfilling? If not, why not?
3. Take a personal inventory of your spiritual life. Do you read the Bible regularly? Could you improve or be more consistent? How is your prayer life? Do you pray daily? Do you attend church regularly? Be honest with yourself.

Prayer

I come before you Lord in full commitment to your principles and precepts. I want to obey all of your commands. I want to show you my love through obedience to your Word. Do not let me falter or stray away. I set my eyes upon you for there's nothing I desire more than to be with you. I seek only the things that pertain to you knowing that if I seek you first all else will be added unto me. Lord, I stand on your Word. In Jesus' name. Amen.

Reflection

_____

_____

_____

_____

_____

A New Start

"Jesus declared "I tell you the truth,
no one can see the Kingdom of God unless
he is born again." (John 3:3)

Many people and nations today are seeking restoration. We want our broken bodies to be whole. People desire broken relationships to be mended. Nations desire that their broken bodies (the people) be restored to peace and prosperity too. The link to what once was and what is has been broken and needs to be restored. Yet, God did not settle for restoration. Rather, he sent His son, Jesus Christ, to bring regeneration. A totally new way of living – a new life.

This point is well-illustrated in the story of Nicodemus. (John 3:1-7) You remember Nick. He was a Pharisee of rare character. He was honestly seeking God's truth. (Ibid) At first he argued that there was no way possible for a baby to re-enter his mother's womb and be reborn. (John 3:4) Initially, he did not understand. What Jesus was referring to was a spiritual rebirth – an entirely new awakening. Jesus was referring to a brand new way of relating to life that is possible only through a change in one's nature. (John 3:7)

The Bible says, "[I]f any is in Christ, he is a new creation; the old has gone, the new has come!" (2 Cor. 5:17) The old nature was focused on self. The new nature is focused on God. You cannot possibly be physically born in this world twice. Your mother only gives birth to you once to be sure. But, you can experience a spiritual birth once you commit your life to Christ. And then, you must nurture the fresh newness you've received. You must nourish yourself through reading God's Word. You must exercise your spiritual muscles by acting on what God asks you to do. You must trust God that things of the past are gone – and you have a new start because you have been born again.

Are you experiencing brokenness in your life? If so, are you ready to experience a brand new way of living? Are you ready to give your life to Jesus today? To experience true change you must be born again.

Affirmation

Father, A New Start:
- Changes how I see who I am
- Helps me look forward not backward
- Changes how I live my life everyday
- Helps me truly know who you are
- Changes how I see whose I am

Meditation Verse

"Sing to the Lord a new song for he has done marvelous things." (Psalm 98:1)

Discussion Questions

1. Are there some areas of your life where you are hurting? Experiencing brokenness? Share with someone you trust. What are you going

through? How did you get to this point? How will you recover?

2. Do you have sin in your life that you've not confessed? If so, are you ready to share every detail with someone today? With God?

3. Read John 3:16 and other verses that you find helpful.

Prayer

Father, I desire to receive you in my heart. I accept that you are the God that I want to serve. I want you to be Lord in my life. I confess that I am a sinner in need of your wonderful grace. I desire your salvation. I believe that Jesus Christ died on the cross for all of my sins – past, present, and future. I pray that as I receive you that you would bless me in ways I never imagined. I love you, Lord. And it's in Jesus' mighty name I pray. Amen.

Reflection

_____

_____

_____

_____

_____

I AM WONDERFULLY MADE

"For you created my inmost being; you knit me together in my mother's womb. I praise you because I am fearfully and wonderfully made." (Psalm 139:13-14)

Some men go through life with the wrong view of themselves because of something that's happened in their past. Your parents did not love one another when you were born so you don't believe you were conceived in love. Your parents divorced soon after your birth and you believe that you were the cause of the divorce. Your parents were not married when you were born and you were a "oops baby" as we say in the world. You suffered some sort of abuse or neglect at the hand of a friend or relative. You had a bad relationship with a parent or stepparent. You were mistreated in some other way as a child.

Well, despite what anyone else might say or think know that you are loved and you are special is God's eyes. You weren't some random person who entered this world. You weren't singled out to have to endure harsh suffering. You were (and are) a beloved child who was wanted and planned long before even time began. You were created for a specific purpose in this world and God has a special plan in mind for you! (Psalm 139: 13-14)

The Bible tells us about how David responded when he accepted this truth. David rejoiced and celebrated in how God created him. He said, "[Y]our works are wonderful." (Ps. 139:14) He traded in his sorrows and shame, and thoughts of low self-worth for believing God fully. "I know that full well" (Ibid). David celebrated the care and detail God took in creating all of who he was. He was overwhelmed by God's goodness and power. "Such knowledge is too wonderful for me." (Ps. 139:6) David did not hesitate to give God praise for what he did. "I praise you because I am fearfully and wonderfully made. (Ps. 139:14)

Do you have a low view of yourself? Has something happened in your past to cause you difficulty in how you see yourself? Do you know how God sees you? If not, then be like David and say, "Search me, O God, and know my heart; test me and know my anxious thoughts. See if there is any offensive way in me, and lead me in the way everlasting." (Ps. 139:23-24)

Affirmation

God, I Am Wonderfully Made:
- No matter what happened in the past
- No matter what other people say
- No matter how I might feel today
- No matter if I have been abused
- Because you created me

Meditation Verse

"May your unfailing love come to me, Oh Lord." (Ps.119:41)

Discussion Questions

1. Has something traumatic happened in your past? A situation that has been difficult to talk about or share with others? Is it time to talk to a Christian counselor, pastor, or close confidant? Is it time for you to confront this situation head on?

2. Is there currently someone in your life that you have not forgiven? Think about that person right now. Should you forgive them? (See Col. 3:13) Will you forgive that person right now?

3. Think about five strengths that you love concerning how God made you. Share the things you've identified with someone or in a small group. Meditate on Psalm 139:13-14.

Prayer

Lord God, I read in your Word that everything you created is 'good.' And, I thank you that I am part of your creation. I am 'good' simply because you said so. Thank you for making me just the way I am. Even if I am not fully confident with every aspect of my life, I trust that you love me just the way I am. You made me and I am loved in your eyes. I need not worry what anyone else says or thinks. I need not worry about anything I've had to endure. Your Word stands true alone. Because you've made me a wonderful creation. I praise you in Jesus' name. Amen.

Reflection

_____

_____

_____

_____

_____

You Are the Boss

"And we pray this in order that you may live
a life worthy of the Lord and may please
him in everyway." Colossians 1:10

How do you know you are doing well on your
job? Either you get promoted or you get a salary
increase. You are commended by your co-workers
or your boss gives you a great evaluation. Whatever
your experience has been there is always some
means by which you can gauge whether you have
been successful or not. But, how do you measure
your success with God?

Paul tells us in Colossians 1:10 that there are at
least three ways we can measure: 1) by bearing fruit
in every good work; 2) by growing in the knowledge
of God; and 3) by being strengthened with all power.
(Col. 1:10-11) Paul says, you can know that you are
living a life worthy of the Lord by the fruit you bear
in this life, how you grow spiritually by not only
reading the Bible, but doing what the Word says, and
how you are light in a dark world. Paul says that you
do these things, in part, for yourself that you might
have patience and great endurance. But, ultimately, it
is so you may please the Lord every day.

Living a life worthy of the Lord doesn't mean
that promotions, salary increases, and praise from
our co-workers and boss are not important. They are.
Those things add value and meaning to our life here
on earth. But, what's most important to God is that

we be a walking epistle in the work place. It's more important that others see that we aren't lazy or regularly tardy to work. It's important for others see we are not competing for a title or position, but rather achieving things because we have the right attitude. We want our co-workers to see us differently.

At the end of the day, you must realize that you are working for God, not men. If you work as if working unto the Lord, then He will be glorified. If you work with right attitude and perspective, then others will notice and see the goodness in you. God is calling you to live a life worthy of what He has called you to be - pleasing to Him in every way.

Affirmation

Lord, You Are The Boss:
- So I let my light shine for my co-workers
- So I do excellent work that glorifies you
- So I do not rob time from you at work
- So I make it a habit to be at work on time
- So I don't lie, cheat, or steal to get ahead

Meditation Verse

And whatever you do, whether in word or deed, do it all in the name of the Lord Jesus, giving thanks to God the Father through Him." (Col. 3:17)

Discussion Questions

1. Do you have a boss at work that has it out for you? Perhaps, s/he doesn't like you or wants to show you who's the boss? Are you a light to him or her or do you give back the same

attitude that's given to you? How can you adjust your attitude in difficult situations? Explain.

2. Are you working for God at work? Do you waste time? Do you share encouraging words with others? Do you work diligently? What would non-believers say about you in the workplace? Are you making a difference for time and eternity?

3. Why does it seem more difficult to be a Christian in the workplace than in church?

Prayer

Lord Jesus, you are sovereign and supreme. You reign over the entire universe. You are Lord over my life. I pray that I would be obedient to you everyday. I don't want to be lazy or late to work. I don't want to lie, cheat, or steal to get ahead. I don't want to step on others for a position or promotion. I do want to be wholly pleasing to you. I do want to be without stain or blemish. I do want to have a pure heart. God, you are the boss. I will follow your lead. In Jesus' name. Amen.

Reflection

_____

_____

_____

_____

_____

FILL ME UP

"Whosoever is thirsty, let him come; and whoever wishes, let him take the free gift of the water of life." (Revelation 22:17)

Has there ever been a time when you were thirsty? Nearly every human being has experienced a time when they were thirsty. Maybe you went on a long walk or you just finished jogging or playing a game. Eventually, you became dehydrated and needed to quench your thirst. You couldn't wait to have something to drink. And, man, when it went down it sure tasted so good. It replenished your supply. It made you feel better. It gave you more energy. But, what you didn't realize was that you needed to fill up again and again and again. The liquid intake we need only temporarily replenishes our diminished supply of fluid. It eventually runs out and we have to fill up each time we run low.

The heavenly Father, however, has an unlimited supply of living water that He offers to us for free. He says, "Come, all you are thirsty." (Rev. 22:17, Isa. 55:1, John 7:37) To you who are thirsty I will give you drink. (Rev. 21:6) And, never again will you thirst. (Rev. 7:16) God wants you to come to Him. He wants you to thirst for Him. "As a deer pants for streams of water, so my soul pants for you, O God. My soul thirsts for God, for the living God." (Psa. 42:1-2) God wants you to have a deep desire to encounter Him. "When can I go and meet with

God?" (Psa. 42:2) God is a Rock and a Redeemer. "[Y]ou will fill me with joy." (Ps. 16:11)

If you haven't experienced the Living God, then it's time to trade in your drink for the living water he has to offer. Your drink is designed for temporary satisfaction. But, what God has will last you a lifetime. If you've never tasted what God has for you won't you give Him a try? And, if you have already accepted him in your heart, do you need him to fill up your cup again? God doesn't want you to just take a sip from his cup. He wants you to taste His goodness everyday because his living water is overflowing. He wants you to have more energy, more power, and a sustained relationship with Him.

Are you feeling dehydrated? Do you need to replenish your water supply? Have you turned to the Source that has the richest water supply? How about taking a drink today?

Affirmation
God, Fill Me Up:
- With your Word
- In my prayer time
- At Sunday service
- During my Bible study
- With your love

Meditation Verse
"Whoever believes in me, as the Scripture has said, streams of living water will flow from within him." (John 7:38)

Discussion Questions

1. Do you read the Bible daily? How does God's Word fill you up? List at least three ways that you get filled up with the Word.
2. Has your spiritual walk with the Lord dried up? How can you get things back on track? What do you need to get back on the right track? What steps do you need to take?
3. Meditate on John 7:38.

Prayer

Praise the Lord. How good and fitting it is to praise you, God. How sweet and pleasant it is to praise your name. Great are you in your might and power. I sing to you with thanksgiving and make music to you with a harp. I will delight in you and put my hope in your unfailing love. You are great and greatly to be praised. In Jesus' name. Amen.

Reflection

_____

_____

_____

_____

_____

9 781607 918967